Luangwa

Memories of Eden

This book is dedicated to Jesus the author and finisher of
my faith.
I would like to thank my wife Kay and my daughter
Kathleen for their patience as I collected the material for
this book.
Special thanks to Andrea Bizzaro and Mfuwe Lodge for
their hospitality and encouragement throughout the project.
To Phil, Ishmail, Keennan, uncle Mike and Mark for their
invaluable stories, and their enthusiasm to get involved.
To Andy and Brendon for allowing me the use of some of
their material.
To John Thomson for his computer skills.
To Linda Bloomfield for always being available to sort out
my text
To Dan Lee for his expertise.
To all the buyers of my paintings, their patronage has
allowed me to carry on with my profession.
To all the people who subscribed to this book, thank you
for your trust.

A Tribute to Norman Joseph Carr

1912:- Norman was born in Chinde on 19th July 1912. Chinde was a British concession in Portugese territory used for the transit of goods from ocean going ships into Zambezi river paddle steamers destined for Nyasaland.

1919:- He was sent off to school in England to, by his own admission, unremarkable academic acclaim.

1930:- He returned to a varied career in Nyasaland including the hunting of garden raiding elephants, and on the basis of this experience was appointed.

1939:- Norman became elephant Control Officer to replace the legendary Charlie Ross whose own career had been terminated by one of his quarry. He was posted to the Luangwa Valley at this time.

1940:- Norman served with the Kings African Rifles in the Abyssinian campaign attaining the rank of Captain.

1944:- On his return he was absorbed into the newly formed Game Department as one of their first Game Rangers in the Luangwa Valley.

1950:- Norman initiated a far-reaching, even visionary concept, by involving the local people in wildlife conservation and by their benefiting financially there from. He encouraged Senior Chief Nsefu Camp was built which was the first game camp open to the public in Northern Rhodesia. Revenue from the camp was paid directly to the Kunda Native Authority.

1951:- Norman was instrumental in organising the first formal professional Hunting Safaris, which were run by the Game Department.

1956:- He retired as Chief Ranger for health reasons after a spinal operation resulting from a buffalo injury.1957:- He was recalled from retirement as warden to develop the Kafue National Park.

1958:- Norman acquired two orphaned lion cubs, the raising of which resulted in the book and subsequent film 'Return to the Wild.'

1961:- The two lions now mature males, were released into the North Luangwa National Park where he saw them a year later, thus concluding a successful rehabilitation into the wild. He finally retired from government and started a private safari operation at Lion Camp. These were the first conducted game viewing tours in Northern Rhodesia. He also initiated guided walking safaris, which became known as wilderness trails. These were very popular and have since been emulated throughout Southern Africa.

1962:- In partnership with Peter Hankin, Norman started Luangwa Safaris, the first hunting safari company.

1963:- Norman was operating out of 'old' Mfuwe camp, collecting visitors from Fort Jameson airport.

1964:- This was the year Zambia gained its independence. Norman moved to the 'new' Mfuwe Lodge.

1968:- He operated walking safaris out of numerous bush camps in the northern areas of the park.

1971:- Norman established the original Chibembe camp in the park.

1975:- Norman built the new Chibembe Safari Camp.

1977:- Chinzombo camp was started s a green season extension to Chibembe.

1979:- Norman initiated and devoted two years to the 'Save the Rhino' campaign in an effort to combat the rampant poaching that was sweeping through the valley.

1981:- He worked as a freelance tour guide while building Kapani Lodge over several years.

1986:- His Excellency Dr. K. D. Kaunda opened Kapani Lodge. Norman worked hard establishing Kapani as a prime tourist destination.

1993:- His last years were spent largely on welfare and charitable projects. He assisted a great many children in primary, Secondary and further education through the Kapani School Fund. He devoted himself to awakening in young people an awareness of wildlife conservation and its importance to their future.

Norman Carr died on 1st April 1997, aged 84.

Decorations and Awards

Zambia	Grand Order of Distinguished Service
U.K.	M.B.E.
W.W.F.	Member of Honour

Publications

Return to the Wild	Collins 1962
The White Impala	Collins 1969
Common Trees and Shrubs of the Luangwa Valley	1978
Valley of the Elephants	Collins 1980
Guide to Wildlife of the Luangwa Valley	1987
'Kakuli'	CBC 1996

Voluntary Conservation Work

Honorary Wildlife Ranger	1961 – 1985
Wildlife Conservation Society of Zambia	
Founder Member and Honorary Life President	
Save the Rhino Trust	
Trustee and first Chairman of Operations Committee	

Text Contributions
by

Philip Berry
Ishmail Osman
Keennan Thole
Michael Ronaldson
Mark Sprong
David Kelly

Published by David Kelly

First Published January 2004
ISBN **0-9546620-0-8**

Copyright ©   David Kelly

Layout by **David Kelly**.
Photography and Scanning by Redwood
Printed and bound by Rotolito Lombarda Italy

Most of the paintings in the book are available as Limited Edition prints of 250 and can be ordered through the following
e-mail address.. kelly@liwonde.fsnet.co.uk

Subscribers:

1) Doris & Randy McCourt
2) Danielle & Mark Typinski
3) Toby McCourt.
4) Grahame & Anne Cousins
5) Simon & Shanie
6) Passoni Family
7) Passoni Family
8) Patrick Bonizzi
9) Nicky Bonizzi
10) Dickie Bonizzi
11) Wilderness Safaris
12) William Green
13) Mr.& Mrs. Paul Crossan
14) John & Laurel
15) Lesley & Vernon (Lilongwe 2003)
16) Mark & Angela Sprong
17) Rob & Angela Kilner
18) Des Tennett
19) Hugh & Juliet Saunders
20) Stancom Tobacco Co. (Mw) Ltd
21) Stancom Tobacco Co. (Mw) Ltd
22) Stancom Tobacco Co. (Mw) Ltd
23) Stancom Tobacco Co. (Mw) Ltd
24) Stancom Tobacco Co. (Mw) Ltd
25) Stancom Tobacco Co. (Mw) Ltd
26) Stancom Tobacco Co. (Mw) Ltd
27) Stancom Tobacco Co. (Mw) Ltd
28) Stancom Tobacco Co. (Mw) Ltd
29) Stancom Tobacco Co. (Mw) Ltd
30) Stancom Tobacco Co. (Mw) Ltd

31) Stancom Tobacco Co. (Mw) Ltd
32) Stancom Tobacco Co. (Mw) Ltd
33) Stancom Tobacco Co. (Mw) Ltd
34) Stancom Tobacco Co. (Mw) Ltd
35) Stancom Tobacco Co. (Mw) Ltd
36) Stancom Tobacco Co. (Mw) Ltd
37) Steve, Kathy & Amy Bowler
38) Arnold & Elsie Bowler
39) Alan &Clare Pitman
40) Mr. A. Barron
41) Mr. A. Barron
42) Simon &Heather Wallace
43) Bill & Liz Rowe-Roberts
44) Mark &Robyn Rowe-Roberts
45) Valerie J. Seekings
46) Bruce & Doreen Barron
47) Clive & Bridget Le Patourel
48) Mick Gange-Harris
49) Mick Gange-Harris
50) Mick Gange-Harris
51) Mick Gange-Harris
52) British Airways
53) British Airways
54) British Airways
55) British Airways
56) British Airways
57) British Airways
58) British Airways
59) British Airways
60) British Airways
61) British Airways
62) Sally Peck
63) Kevin & Raoffa Kelly
64) Sue & Paul Alves

65) John & Lynne Royle
66) Ian & Catriona Morgan
67) Alan Ralph Robson
68) Lois & Giorgio Losacco
69) Tony & Joanne Faulkner
70) Bert & June Van der Merwe
71) Zayne, Kyle & Shaun Van der Merwe
72) Charlie & Dorothy Clark
73) The Graham Family
74) Pat & Tony Pain
75) Chris Pain
76) Dimon (Mw) Ltd
77) Dimon (Mw) Ltd
78) Dimon (Mw) Ltd
79) Dimon (Mw) Ltd
80) Dimon (Mw) Ltd
81) Dimon (Mw) Ltd
82) Dimon (Mw) Ltd
83) Dimon (Mw) Ltd
84) Dimon (Mw) Ltd
85) Dimon (Mw) Ltd
86) Nick & Wendy Marshall
87) Costantini Anna
88) Costantini Linda
89) Jess & Ade
90) Sheena & Patrick
91) Heather Mansfield
92) Julia Kemp
93) Africaleaf (Mw) Ltd
94) Africaleaf (Mw) Ltd
95) Africaleaf (Mw) Ltd
96) Africaleaf (Mw) Ltd
97) Africaleaf (Mw) Ltd
98) Africaleaf (Mw) Ltd

99) Africaleaf (Mw) Ltd
100) Africaleaf (Mw) Ltd
101) Africaleaf (Mw) Ltd
102) Africaleaf (Mw) Ltd
103) Margaret & Stewart Anton
104) Sheila & Tina
105) Leon & Wendy Swart
106) Marijam Jones
107) Charles & Sheena Carey
108) David &Ruth Lee
109) Mike & Anne Mcphun
110) Marian Yun
111) Heather & Jonathan Kneeshaw
112) Gavin & Jane Lockhead
113) Gavin & Jane Lockhead
114) Margaret Lockhead
115) Dieter & Esther Gringinger
116) Tim & Nicola
117) Mr. & Mrs. Cruz
118) Gillian Mann
119) Gerard Grant
120) John & Sandra Paton
121) Jonathan & Heather Kneeshaw
122) Elio & Grazia Bizzaro
123) Gianluca & Alessandra Bizzaro
124) Giuseppe & Rosaria Bizzaro
125) Alessandra Bizzaro
126) Benedetto Mariano
127) Maria Letizia
128) Franco
129) Tony & Crystal Hawken
130) Tony & Crystal Hawken
131) Peter & Alvena Grant
132) Eddie Fitch
133) Tim & Nicola de Borde

134) Andy Hogg & Alison Oliver
135) Trish & John Berry
136) John Burdett & Warwick Hoffman
137) Craig MacRae
138) Chris Worden
139) David & Carolyn Tett & Elizabeth Player
138) Molly Care
139) Phil Berry & Babette Alfieri
140) Oriana Morgante & Andrea Bizzaro
141) Mfuwe Lodge- " The Norman Carr Memorial Library"
142) Umberto & Letizia Bizzaro
143) Mr. & Mrs. Morgante
144) Club Makokola
145) Michael & Eileen Kelly
146) Margaret Black
147) Mike, Sally, Sarah & Amanda Roberts
148) Mike & Bridget Gibbs
149) Mr. & Mrs. S. Carr

Contents:

Carmine Bee-eaters

Map of the South Luangwa National Park

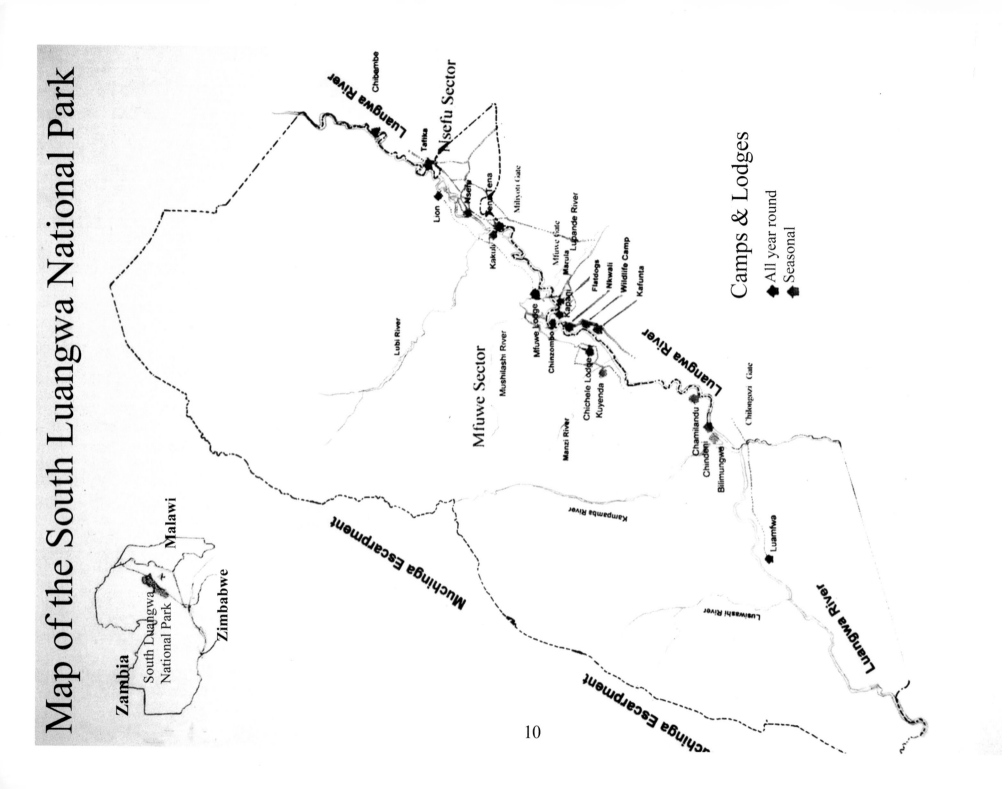

FOREWORD

For an artist, the Luangwa Valley is the ultimate studio for it is full of life, colour, light and shadow. It abounds with wonderful subjects, most notably the prolific game animals - leopards for which the Valley is renowned, elephants wading the river, great herds of buffalo, hordes of hippo, lion prides, dambos filled with puku, impala and zebra, and many more. Then there are the hundreds of bird species, of which many are feathered jewels displaying the brilliant colours of the rainbow. But apart from all these creatures, there is also tremendous variety in the splendid wild landscapes, the magnificent trees and golden grasslands. There is so much from which to choose that a painter could be kept busy with brush and palette for many a year. Surprisingly, only a handful of artists, some very well-known, have painted in the Valley and none until now has ever published his or her work in a single book devoted solely to the Luangwa.

Now with this beautiful volume of his paintings, David Kelly is pioneering new horizons and at the same time setting a very high standard for other artists to emulate. David has a keen eye for detail and his superb and accurate portrayals of the wildlife and scenery, the safari camps, and the people of the Valley are very evocative. He has truly captured the spirit of the Valley in scenes that are quintessentially Luangwa.

For anyone who loves the Luangwa Valley, this is a book to treasure, for it will bring back with nostalgia vivid memories of this magnificent wilderness. David has created a wonderful tribute to the Luangwa which will surely enhance its reputation as one of the best of Africa's wild Edens.

Philip Berry
Mfuwe, Luangwa Valley

Introduction

I believe that the Garden of Eden really existed, and that several beauty spots of this world were a part of it. The beauty of the Luangwa has drawn me back again and again. Its varying landscape, space and abundant wildlife species are a nature lover's paradise.

I first learned of this sanctuary from my parents. They had visited my uncle who worked as a game ranger in the late 50s through to the early 60s. From my very first visit I appreciated what had generated such an enthusiasm in my parents as they described its beauty.

Artists like David Sheperd, whose great efforts in conservation have brought the welfare of endangered species to the fore, mainly inspired my passion for wildlife art.

Two years after deciding to put together work for the Luangwa book, I was elated to hear that Phil Berry, a man my uncle occasionally mentioned, was still working as a safari guide. I looked forward to meeting Phil so that I would be able to tie up a few loose ends.

Andrea Bizzaro, owner of Mfuwe Lodge invited me to stay at his lodge as I set out to achieve this vision. On mentioning a possible meeting with Phil. Andrea told me what a private man Phil was and that he avoided the limelight. Phil would be in camp the following day and would see what he could organize.

I met Phil Berry the following day. He greeted me with a broad infectious smile, which broadened further when I mentioned my uncle Mike. Yes, they had worked together 40 years previously. When I mentioned Ishmail Osman, he laughed and asked how the scallywag was doing. I told Phil of my intended project and asked if he would be involved. He did become involved and I am very grateful.

I decided to take Ishmail into the valley to try and relive some of his enthusiasm with him. It was fun. As providence would have it, Phil was in camp and they met up. Phil's first words were 'Ishmail, you look like a muzungu madala (old white man)', referring to Ishmail's graying beard.

After they exchanged updates of their lives, Phil turned and explained to me how Ishmail had accumulated about 30 pairs of hiking boots in one season. He deliberately wore old worn out boots, and clients would take pity on him, leaving their seven day old, bought specially for the trip boots with him. They continued to chat, laughter forming a great part of the conversation. I had moved away to give them some privacy, and when they parted, Ishmail came over to me. He told me what fun it was seeing Phil again after such a long time. He then added, 'you know David, Phil used to be such a good-looking chap.' Now it was my turn to laugh.

I later introduced Ishmail to Keennan, one of the senior guides at Mfuwe. They got on well, and we had a few very fruitful game drives together. I soaked in their experience, their bush craft and knowledge. I was surprised to find out that Keennan knew my uncle, even if it was from a different type of watering hole. They drank at the same bottle store, or pub, in Makeni, Lusaka. The picture was almost complete.

Woodland Kingfisher

Chapter 1

Enter Mfuwe

Mfuwe main gate is situated right by the Luangwa bridge. Your arrival will be met by pleasent staff, who work for the Zambia Widlife Authority.Clement Mwaimbolwa has worked here for thirteen years

Above - Hippo Foot print

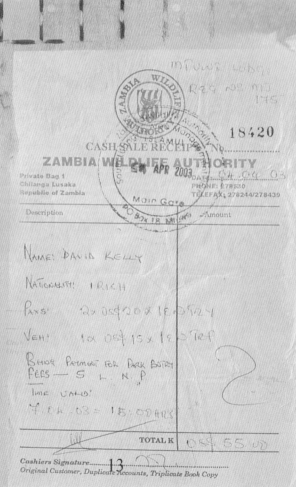

Clement Mwaimbolwa

It's mid afternoon and hot.

Facing page- *The chief in his stride*

15

Scene from the Luangwa bridge looking North

Greeted by a welcoming committee of Elephant.

Mfuwe Lodge-*A first sighting of the magnificent Mfuwe Lodge. The chalets look out onto lagoons that are rich with wildlife. A blessing for those who like to potter around - not moving very far.*

David – Kelly

Grey Lourie

Baobab Tree

This Baobab acts as a marker when you are looking for Mfuwe Lodge. You turn right soon after passing the tree and you will see a wooden carved sign written 'Mfuwe Lodge'. The Baobab trees found in the park form a part of the extremely varied and rich vegetation the park has to offer.

Mfuwe Lodge

MFUWE LODGE

THE INEVITABLE END
NO CEREMONIES

This family of warthog were nibbling on the new grass shoots
of the irrigated Mfuwe grounds. The little ones were a little
skittish, but soon settled down and followed their mother's
example.

20

The stairs up and through the reception area do not seem to deter this family of six elephant from getting at the wild mango tree in the courtyard. As they passed the reception desk, one of them stretched it's trunk over the desk with the hope of finding a tasty morsel of food. You do have to remain alert as you walk around the lodge grounds, there is no restricted access to the wildlife, and therefore there is always something to see.

Right- This irate elephant charged our vehicle because it thought we were a threat to its young calf. I took this shot whilst weak at the knees with fear.

As the day draws to a close the light changes dramatically. It is noticeable that everything is shutting down and giving an opportunity for the creatures of the night to take the stage. This hippo, quite unsure of his safety, is staying close to the river until we move away from the area. Hippos like to come out at dusk and will feed throughout the night.

Wafwa Sunset

CHAPTER 2
FORTY YEARS IN THE SOUTH LUANGWA
By Philip Berry

As a consequence of having lived and worked in and around the Luangwa Valley during the past forty years I am often asked what changes I have witnessed in that time. Inevitably, there have been many over the years especially in the South Luangwa National Park, Zambia's premier wildlife sanctuary and the scene of most of my service in the valley in wildlife conservation and safari guiding.

I first set foot in the South Luangwa Game Reserve (it was not a National Park then) on the first day of April, 1963. It was not an auspicious arrival fated perhaps because it was April Fools Day! Peter Morris, the senior ranger responsible for the Reserve, was taking me by Landrover to the sector headquarters at Lusangazi which I was to take over from the incumbent ranger, Mike Slogrove, who was transferring to the Kafue National Park in western Zambia. After passing through the entrance gate at Kanzutu and halfway to Lusangazi the vehicle sank to its axles in black glutinous mud, so typical of the clay soils in the valley's extensive mopane woodlands. Despite all our efforts we were unable to extricate the vehicle and had to spend the night there. Early the next morning, Peter sent one of the game guards who were with us, walking to Lusangazi and eventually a tractor came to tow our vehicle out.

Lusangazi camp, then both a ranger station and a small tourist camp, was situated just inside the game reserve at the confluence of the Luangwa and Lusangazi rivers. With superb views of the Luangwa river, especially downstream where the sun setting over the distant Muchinga Escarpment was reflected in molten gold in the river's waters, Lusangazi was the headquarters for the southern half of the South Reserve and the controlled hunting areas outside its boundaries.

The two sectors of the reserve for which I was responsible were the Chilongozi

23

Chief

We might as well not have been there, that's how ignored we felt when looking at this magnificent male lion. We soon found out why he was paying us no mind, there was an attractive lady lion we hadn't seen on the other side of our vehicle. He was courting and to him we weren't a threat, just a nuisance.

and Serenje sectors. Except for one road to Kaumba camp at the base of the Muchingas and a rough track to the upper Kapamba River there were no roads in the latter sector.

The Chilongozi sector, though, was better served with roads to the game guard boundary camps and several game-viewing roads for tourists. There were a total of twelve game guard posts around the boundaries of my sectors plus another two in the hunting areas outside. Each post was staffed with two guards or, rarely, three and one carrier to carry their food and blankets on long patrols. The wives and children also lived in the camps. Most of the outposts in the Serenje sector could only be reached on foot which entailed my undertaking foot safaris (ulendo) of one or two weeks duration to visit and check the camps. In those days, though poaching occurred in the reserve, it was not a major problem and two guards in each boundary post making regular patrols were sufficient to maintain reasonable control over poaching incursions.

In any event, most of the poaching was for meat, especially buffalo and warthog, and the weapons used were mostly homemade muzzle-loading guns. The game stocks in the reserve were good so poaching then did not have a serious impact on animal numbers. It was only in the mid-1970's when the price of ivory and rhino horn on the black market reached astronomically high levels, that poaching became a serious problem. Then the poaching gangs became much bigger and more aggressive and they were better armed, often with semiautomatic rifles. In this new situation the two-man guard posts became impractical and ineffective. Two guards could not be expected to challenge and arrest gangs of 15 or 20 poachers so virtually all the boundary camps around the South Reserve were closed down and the staff withdrawn to the main ranger stations.

For me, though, my years as a ranger in the South Reserve were a wonderful time the memories of which I shall always cherish. It was a hard life but I was young and fit and anxious to learn as much as possible about the huge area for which I was responsible. The reserve held many wild and secret places; magnificent trees and beautiful rivers, and an abundance and great diversity of wild creatures so for me it was a time of exploration and exciting discovery. Nevertheless, the duties of a ranger entailed working long hours each day covering a wide spectrum of activities.

The administration of my area included supervision of the game guards, patrolling the reserve, visiting the boundary camps, the maintenance and operation of two self-catering tourist camps (Chilongozi and Lusangazi), wildlife surveys, the grading and upkeep of tourist roads, law enforcement and anti-poaching,

and the shooting of three or four buffalo a month to feed the staff and their families including the construction and road maintenance crews. In addition, outside the reserve my responsibilities covered the control shooting of elephants and other animals that were a danger to life or destructive of crops and property, and to regularly check licenced hunting parties in the hunting areas.

There were five officers responsible for the South Reserve. Three were based in Fort Jameson (now Chipata) the headquarters of the Game Department's Luangwa Command. Apart from Peter Morris, these were Bill Bullock the Warden, and Frank Ansell the wildlife biologist; all three were long serving and very experienced game officers. Then there was Mike Ronaldson, stationed at Mfuwe, who was the ranger in charge of the northern half of the South Reserve. Finally, there was myself; as assistant game ranger I was the junior officer and very low in the ranks!

The game guards were for the most part a fine body of men. Though, to a large degree, they had only a limited education they were nearly all skilled in bushcraft and the ways of wild animals. They had been recruited because of these very qualities. Many were also ex-soldiers who had served in various campaigns during the Second World War in the Northern Rhodesia Regiment and the King's African Rifles. They were well disciplined and proud of their regimental backgrounds, which they carried on into their quasi-military service as game guards. Some had also been trained as elephant control guards (hunters) or fundis as they were locally known. This was a position that gave the fundis a measure of prestige amongst the villagers outside the reserve whose lives and crops they had to try and protect against marauding elephants, lions, buffalo and other dangerous animals.

Some were exceptionally outstanding men such as Wailo Chiwalo who was my senior game scout and who won the Military Medal for gallantry fighting the Japanese in Burma; Ngambilani Mwenda, more often known as Katalila, also an ex-soldier and a superb elephant hunter who rarely used more than one cartridge to kill a crop-raiding elephant. There were Andulufu Banda, a fine guard who was not afraid to patrol alone in the bush, a trait that years later led to his being murdered by poachers, Reuben Lutoba, one of my head game guards, a crusty-natured but nevertheless excellent man to be with in the bush, and many more of similar calibre.

I had great respect and admiration for these men who were the backbone of the Game Department's role in anti-poaching and wildlife conservation. Without them the task would have proved impossible. In the present day and age, although there

Thornicroft's Giraffe

a radical change: the earlier guards wore shorts and a short-sleeved bush jacket both in jungle green, an Australian- style stiff-brimmed bush bat buttoned up on the left side making it easy to slope arms with a rifle without dislodging the hat, a leather belt, black leather boots, and a pair of puttees to wind around and protect the lower legs. Nowadays the scouts' uniform is very similar to that of a soldier's with long trousers, a shirt and a small, golfer's cap all in a jungle green colour. The present-day uniform does not distinguish scouts as wildlife personnel like the old uniform did.

I remember well how the "old" guards used to turn out on morning parade when they were to be inspected by me or another ranger. Their bush jackets and shorts were well starched and ironed with a knife-edge crease in the shorts. They were generally a proud, well-drilled and disciplined body of men. Though naturally some did not come up to the required standards on parade those usually had other important qualities like expertise in anti-poaching investigations or outstanding bush skills as hunters and trackers.

Whenever time and the routine duties of a ranger permitted, I would tour the remoter areas of my sectors on foot visiting the game guard camps, carrying out wildlife surveys and checking on poaching activities. Each tour was usually of between one and two weeks duration and I would be accompanied by two or three guards and a number of porters who carried our food and bedding. I regarded these foot safaris as one of the most enjoyable aspects of my job. There is a wonderful sense of freedom about walking in remote trackless bush amongst all kinds of wild creatures far from human habitation. The fact that my job as a ranger was to help in protecting and conserving for posterity the wildlife and the beautiful habitats in which they lived was very satisfying, and made the occasional hardships all seem worthwhile.

In 1963, the South Luangwa was still very wild and in its infancy as a tourist destination. There were only six small self-catering camps: Chilongozi and Lusangazi , Mfuwe camp, Nsefu (in what was then Chief Nsefu's private game reserve), and Lion and Big Lagoon camps. Six camps where there are now 30 lodges and camps in the same area! None of the camps had more than 12 beds. Visitors used their own vehicles for game viewing and brought their own food. The Game Department provided camp staff including a cook, and all the bedding and equipment. There was also an

are some outstanding wildlife scouts (the title introduced in the 1970's to replace that of "game guard") there are few who are equal to those guards with whom I worked 40 years ago. Even the uniforms have undergone

26

armed escort guard at each camp who was available to take visitors walking amongst the wildlife. In the rains, when the tourist camps were closed, these guards resumed their other duties as control fundis, shooting crop-raiding elephants and other marauding dangerous animals. In those days there were few safari guides in the valley (other than Norman Carr and his few assistants operating his specialized walking safaris) and it speaks well of the expertise and training of the escort guards that no visitor was ever injured by a wild animal on these walks accompanied only by a fundi.

of the wet season although when the three main tributaries (the Lutembwe, Lupande and Matizye) were in flood these prevented access by vehicle during the peak of the rains. To facilitate access, Mike Ronaldson, the ranger at Mfuwe, built a suspension bridge for vehicles across the main problem river, the Lupande. Thick wooden planks were lashed to steel cables that were anchored to trees on either side of the river. It was an ingenious affair but a nightmare to drive a vehicle on because the bridge swayed and pitched alarmingly above the swirling floodwaters of the

Fish Eagle

The game camps as they were known, opened every year in June and closed at the end of October because all the roads were seasonal and once the rains began access was almost impossible. Only the main gravel road from Fort Jameson (Chipata) to Mfuwe pontoon was passable for much

Lupande River! After the first attempt I do not think I ever repeated the experience!

Apart from the seasonal roads, which had to be regraded after the rains had ended in late April, there were also three pontoons that were installed

27

at the same time. The largest, which could carry two vehicles simultaneously, was the Mfuwe pontoon. The others, which took only one vehicle at a time, were at Chibembe in the north and Lusangazi in the south. The two small pontoons were pulled out of the Luangwa River when the rains came to avoid being swept away by the rising floodwaters whereas the Mfuwe pontoon was strongly anchored to the bank but was also inoperable. There was, in addition, another means of access but again only in the dry season: this was the small graded airfield inside the Reserve near the present-day Mfuwe Lodge which was mainly used by Game Department aircraft when carrying out aerial surveys.

It was always an interesting time opening up the Reserve at the beginning of each new tourist season, recruiting temporary workers to repair and renovate the tourist camps, installing the pontoons and grading and hand-hoeing the Reserve's roads. When the big road-grading machines made the new cuts along the overgrown and churned-up roads the newly overturned earth had its own distinctive scent. The grading would expose masses of grass seeds that always attracted great numbers of Cape Turtle and Laughing Doves, guineafowl and francolins taking advantage of the bountiful food supply suddenly available to them. It was always amusing to see the reaction of the impala in particular to the appearance of the newly graded roads. The sudden appearance of cut paths where none had existed for months always confused them and the impala, when running to a road would invariably go soaring over in a single curving bound. Later, when they had become used to the presence of the graded roads, life returned to normal and the impala would merely canter across.

In 1964, Johnny Uys, a Senior Game Ranger, was transferred to the Luangwa Valley to replace Peter Morris and a few months later he was appointed Warden when Bill Bullock retired. Johnny was a legend as a ranger, hunter and naturalist. Leslie Allen was transferred from Mpika and as Senior Ranger, he was second-in-command to Johnny. They were a dynamic duo, Johnny the field officer and Leslie Allen the headquarters administrator, and between them they implemented much-needed reform and expansion of the Game Department's activities in the Valley.

A mobile anti-poaching unit was formed to operate in any part of the Command where poaching was serious, many new roads were constructed in the reserve, and a pilot game cropping scheme was started to find the most efficient way of utilizing the over-abundance of elephant and hippo especially. When Johnny Uys first arrived in the valley he was appalled by the devastation of the habitat by elephants in particular and he was given permission by the Department's Director to carry out an aerial survey of all the Luangwa Game Reserves counting elephant, buffalo and rhino. Along with various other game officers I took a turn in assisting with the counts but at that time of year (October) it was excessively hot and the turbulence made the small single-engine plane bounce about most unpleasantly. The aerial census was the first of its kind ever carried out in Luangwa and after five days of flying many transects, the final results showed the valley held 35,000 elephants of which 15,000 were in the South Reserve.

As a consequence of the census, the government approved the culling of a large number of elephant and hippo, the meat to be sold in the main towns and cities in Zambia. A large and sophisticated cropping station for dissecting the carcasses and packing the refrigerated meat was built near the Mfuwe pontoon outside the Reserve in 1965 and for the next five years the culling continued. Jack Botha was the cropping manager; a brilliant innovator, he was the one who mostly planned and built the cropping station. To facilitate the culling, an extensive network of roads was cut in the South Reserve and also more game-viewing roads were made for visitors. In addition, two new lodges, Mfuwe and Luamfwa, were built to replace the original old Mfuwe and Chilongozi camps respectively.

After being stationed for several years at both Fort Jameson and Mfuwe with active involvement throughout that period with the South Reserve I was transferred away from Luangwa in 1969 to the Game Department's headquarters at Chilanga near Lusaka. Though my official duties took me to the valley from time to time it was not until 1973 when I left the Department that I returned to Luangwa on a permanent basis. Development of the reserve was increasing dramatically because it was now considered to be one of the most important tourist attractions in the country.

There had been many changes during the time I was away. The South Reserve had now become a National Park that also now included the old Nsefu Game Reserve; Chichele Lodge had been built on Kapiri Nkonde Hill; and work was in progress on both the construction of a bridge over the Luangwa to replace the Mfuwe pontoon, and an international airport at Masumba outside the Park. A system of all-weather roads was also being constructed in the Park in the Mfuwe and Chichele areas so that visitors could stay at those lodges and game-view in the rains.

Elephants crossing a dried out dambo

29

My new role was as Safari Manager for the Zambia National Tourist Bureau (a parastatal company) based at Mfuwe. In that capacity, I was required to establish a walking safari operation with a number of small camps to compete with Norman Carr's wilderness trails in the northern Chibembe area of the Park, which were very popular. As a result, after much walking up and down the Luangwa and Kapamba Rivers I chose a site on the former to build Tundwe as our main walking safari camp and placed several small subsidiary tented camps on the Luangwa, Manze and Kapamba Rivers. At the same time I assumed responsibility for all the non-catering camps, Nsefu, Lion, Big Lagoon and Luambe, the latter being in the Luambe Park further up the Luangwa River.

To keep me even busier, all the ZNTB safari guides and game-viewing Land Rovers at the three main lodges, Mfuwe, Chichele and Luamfwa became my responsibility as well! Nevertheless, it was a task I greatly enjoyed for the next three years during which two senior guides ably assisted me. They were James Schultz, the son of Bert Schultz who was a former senior game ranger and legendary hunter in the valley, and Agrippa Mwanza. Because there was now a large increase in tourism to the valley to all the main catering lodges and to both Norman Carr's and the ZNTB walking safaris, Zambia Airways began flying visitors in to the airfield in the Park near Mfuwe Lodge. The aeroplanes used were Hawker Siddeley aircraft which each carried 44 passengers.

In the early 1970's there were enormous numbers of elephants in the South National Park and black rhinos were frequently encountered, almost on a daily basis. A major UN/FAO project to survey wildlife populations in Luangwa and make recommendations to government was carried out over a period of four years from 1970 to 1973. Annual aerial censuses were made of elephant, buffalo and rhino and some startling statistics were announced at the conclusion of the project including 86,000 elephant and at least 4,000 rhinos in the entire valley. Understandably, with so many elephants in the valley the habitats were suffering tremendous damage but, due to much controversy over the pros and cons, the government had stopped the elephant-culling scheme in 1970. No one really realized it at the time but in about 1975 elephant and rhino poaching by sophisticated and heavily armed gangs began in earnest. This unintentionally relieved pressure on the habitats as far as elephants were concerned but the poaching drastically effected the social structure of the herds and destroyed virtually all the adult elephants carrying the largest ivory tusks.

In December 1975, two of the most important changes came into effect when the new international airport at Masumba (but named Mfuwe Airport) and the new bridge over the Luangwa at Mfuwe were opened and became fully operational. In addition, the road between the new airport and the bridge had been tarred for the first time and a sizeable network of all-weather laterite roads had been completed in the South Park. Looking back to twelve years before, I found it difficult to believe the radical changes that had taken place in that time. Where once I had driven my Land Rover in trepidation across the Lupande River on Mike Ronaldson's swaying suspension bridge now I could speed across on a permanent bridge; I could drive across the Luangwa with my vehicle above that river's high and surging floodwaters where previously the pontoon would have been inoperable and, in the Park I could reach places within an hour by vehicle that previously it would have required hard slogging on foot for a day or more to reach.

My contract with ZNTB having been completed in 1976, I accepted an offer from Norman Carr to manage both his recently constructed Chibembe Lodge and his wilderness trails (walking safaris) operation. Norman was the grand old man of conservation in Zambia, a legend in his time, and I was delighted to have the opportunity of working with him. Though running a major lodge was not my ideal, I enjoyed the walking safari side of the job and there were many good friends and colleagues with whom I worked: these included Vernon Baillie, Robin Pope, Ishmail Osman, Clive Kelly and Patrick Ansell to name a few, all very experienced safari guides. Having to keep control of such a varied bunch of scallywags put years on my age but they were all very entertaining and great fun to have around!

By 1977, we were beginning to find signs of elephant poaching to the west of the Chibembe walking safari area; it was now becoming obvious that the wave of ivory and rhino poaching that had begun some years previously in East Africa had now reached the Luangwa Valley. Unfortunately, the National Parks and Wildlife Service (as the Game Department had been renamed) was going through a major crisis lacking sufficient funds, vehicles, equipment and manpower to cope with the poaching problem. As the poaching escalated, Norman once again rose to the occasion. After lobbying the Zambian Government and internationally known conservationists like Sir Peter Scott (of the World Wildlife Fund) and David Shepherd, his efforts resulted in the establishment of the Save the Rhino Trust a non-governmental organisation on the 1~ of January, 1980.

However, while all the bureaucratic wrangling was going on to bring SRT into being, Zambia Safaris, the parent company of Wilderness Trails, had temporarily

Life and death

contributed my services to carry out anti-poaching patrols with teams of wildlife scouts in the Parks. What we found during those early patrols was horrifying: the carcasses of scores of slaughtered elephants and many rhinos with only the ivory or horns having been removed. Sometimes we encountered poaching gangs and captured prisoners and ivory. We also recovered many tusks from elephants that, though mortally wounded, had managed to elude the poachers but died of their wounds later. The poachers were using mostly semi-automatic rifles, which used a lot of ammunition but unless the hunter was an expert shot these weapons tended only to wound an elephant.

Once the Save the Rhino Trust was formally established, Norman asked me if I wished to command the anti-poaching unit on a full-time basis: I would be answerable to an Operations Committee comprised of several of the SRT Trustees and volunteers with himself as chairman. The SRT was a joint project financed by the government (who also provided 22 scouts full-time) and the World Wildlife Fund. I was, of course, delighted because it was not only a very worthwhile endeavour but it also enabled me to revert once again to doing what I had loved years before as a game ranger:

I could criss-cross the Luangwa Parks on foot patrols lasting between one and three weeks tracking down and apprehending poachers and bringing them to justice. It was hard work, often physically debilitating, especially in the rains when malaria, flooding rivers and great expanses of wet, black mud created obstacles to be endured and overcome. It was also hard spiritually and very depressing. Whenever we found slaughtered elephants and rhinos I knew that despite our efforts we were too few in number to adequately patrol and protect the area of nearly 20,000 square kilometres that we had to cover. We had our successes capturing some gangs with various large hauls of ivory (the most from one gang was 48 tusks) and occasionally rhino horns as well. A few poachers were also killed and wounded during some of these encounters.

After serving for a period of four years in charge of the anti-poaching unit in Luangwa I left but continued my connection with SRT by becoming a safari guide at Chinzombo Lodge. SRT purchased the lodge in 1984 from Zambia Safaris with the intention of using the profits from the lodge to fund the continuing operations of the anti-poaching units in the field. This was moderately successful for the next few years but it was clearly evident that unless a really big project with substantial and long-term funding could be implemented ivory and rhino poaching would never be contained. The Norwegian Government fortunately came to the rescue and since 1986 to the present day have financed a conservation project embracing the South Luangwa Park and the adjacent game management (controlled hunting) area. When this project started it took over the anti-poaching function of SRI so this latter organisation no longer carries out any of its former activities in the field.

Now, I am purely a safari guide, still working in the South Luangwa forty years after I first started there. Employed by the Bushcamp Company, which is owned and operated by Andy Hogg and Andrea Bizzaro, I run a small seasonal pole and grass safari bush camp on the Manze River ably assisted by my better half, Babette Alfieri. So many more lodges and small bush camps have sprung up along the Luangwa River in the past 20 years that during the dry season the South Luangwa is a hive of tourist activity. This is obviously good for the tourism industry, the national economy and wildlife conservation. Nevertheless, although much of the South Luangwa is still wild and unspoiled so many changes have occurred during my sojourn in the valley that I often still yearn for those long-ago days when life in the valley was simpler and more idyllic. But, although it is essential to remember the past in order to learn for the future, one must look forward with the hope that any new development of this magnificent Park will be sensitively done, to preserve the integrity of one of Zambia's most precious gems.

Confrontation

Sounds quite dramatic, doesn't it ? I used alot of artistic license to create this image. I was trying to compare the strength of my Unimog with the natural strength of an African bull elephant. The place does exist, but the composition is a figment of my imagination. I have great respect for both the elephant and my Unimog.

Luangwa Wafwa

The South Luangwa National Park cannot be truly depicted without emphasizing it's wide open spaces. The fisheye riverine scenes are breathtakingly beautiful. The landscape constantly changes as the many different wildlife species visit the river for a much needed drink. The picture above is early September when the Carmine Bee-eaters are nesting in it's banks. They constantly fly, gathering insects to feed themselves and their young.The predators they have to look out for are monitor lizzards and birds of prey.

Yellowbilled Storks

Carmine Bee- eaters

Chapter Three

To Lion Camp and beyond

Zebra, Impala and Puku nibble new grass shoots

David-Kelly

Owani Lagoon.- *This lagoon was aptly named from the sound made by the Crested Crane. Whilst the water lasts, the cranes find nourishment here. They share the lagoon with Puku and baboon. The flocks of cranes far outnumber the other animal species. What a sight to behold.*

Dusting- *Elephant wet their bodies and find a dusty patch of ground where they spray the dust over themselves. This forms a hard layer that makes a temporary deterrant against biting insects.*

40

The River is littered with trees and branches brought down by the floods.

Slenderly and gracefully these giraffe cross the dry dambo

The pieces of grass that have attached themselves to this fallen tree give evidence as to what heights the river rises in the wet season.

Lubi River

Studies of elephant behaviour have drawn the conclusion that they have very long memories. The bull elephant that you see on the left engaged in what appears to be a relay race, at a guess was probably in his mid to late twenties. Ismail's attempt to greet an old friend did not quite work out. At twenty metres his gestures seemed far from a warm and friendly greeting, Ishmail had to 'leg it.'

Learning to dust

Kaingo camp is situated between the Lubi river and Lion camp. The camp is owned by Derek Shenton, and is seasonal. It is highly recommended for both it's rustic and yet comfortable accommodation. An American friend of mine stayed here quite alot. There is a good view of the river.

Kaingo camp

Ishmail awaits the delivery of the baton.

Kakuli
(not quite)

Gerard, Duncan and myself were driving across Lion Plain when we came across this fellow. At first it appeared that he was alone, so I shouted "Kakuli!" "Not quite," retorted Duncan, eyes as sharp as ever. Directly behind this buffalo was another and only noticeable when he lifted his head. I opted to paint what I had originally seen. On all my ventures into the Luangwa Valley, I have never seen a lone bull buffalo, always in groups of two to five, or very large herds.

After crossing the Mwamba River on route to Lion Camp, there is a diversion along the river. The picture above shows hippo ready to run into the river in case we pose a threat. Their cautious glances a sign of uncertainty.

Squirrel

Left-*Lion Plain*

We were unable to proceed to Big Lagoon, as the road stopped here. Actually there was a large tree across the road, and the tracks stopped right in front of it.

Lion Camp

Lion Camp has a lovely setting. The camp is seasonal. It is comfortable, and the service is good.

Unfortunately the above view is one I became quite used to. Most of the time they were not prepared to pose for my camera.

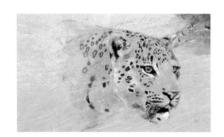

Leopard - *The sightings of these beautiful cats are quite frequent. Though shy, they seem to feel less threatened by the presence of people.*

Chapter Four

Ishmail Osman

I was born on the 22nd November 1945 in Balaka. Nyasaland, now Malawi. I finished my high school education at Sir Robert Armitage High School.

In 1965, I ventured into Zambia to meet one of my heroes in person. I arrived in Chipata and met "The Norman Carr" smoking his favourite Ronson pipe at his office.

As I introduced myself he said "You are a Nyasaland boy, what can I do for you?" I replied that my intention was to meet at least one of my heroes. He laughed with his gaze still fixed on a pair of elephant tusks that were brought in by a professional hunter named Joe Joubert.

Even though I hadn't told him my name, he introduced me to Joe Joubert as one of his new recruits. His exact words were, "Meet my new Brown White Hunter". We all had a good laugh.

NJC went on to ask if I had a driving licence and valid passport, which I produced. That very same day he entrusted me with a new Ford Truck and money to buy provisions in Malawi for the six Hunting Camps, and the New Mfuwe Tourist Camp. However, Joe questioned NJC's immediate trust with both vehicle and money. Realising that Joe's question was based on my skin colour, Norman fumed and said it is time other races became more involved in this predominately white profession. He further backed his argument by using Ranger Mike Ronaldson as an example, whose excellent record with the game department, was both mixed race and from Nyasaland.

I was thrilled by NJC's vote of confidence and started what was to be an enjoyable thirteen years in the Luangwa.

Entrusted with NJC's personal Range Rover, I took camp rations down to Mfuwe Camp. The journey was a very long 130kms from Chipata. Leaving the bright lights of Chipata behind and dressed in new green sleeveless shirt and trousers, a pair of Safari boots with no socks, I headed into the wilderness.

I arrived at the New Pontoon site around 5pm. Hippos were the first to greet me and crossing the Luangwa River for the first time was very exciting. The sun setting over the River is a picture that will always remain in my mind.

I arrived at Mfuwe Camp with its 8 semi-detached chalets, a main dining area and open bar. There were some tourists and two professional hunters, Johnny Roxbrough and Geoff, staying. I had not met these men before and as there was no telephone, my arrival was a total surprise. I introduced myself and after an evening meal and a few beers, we settled down for the night.

Next morning, I introduced myself in Nyanja to the Zambian staff, including the game guards they were delighted that they had an intermediary.

It was a lazy first day and I sat on the main bar veranda watching impala and Puku coming to drink water in the Mfuwe lagoon. As evening grew, NJC arrived in a new Ford Transit with an open roof, no windows, or doors. As the two professional hunters went out to greet him, I was summoned to their meeting. When NJC said that I was to be entrusted with similar duties to theirs, there was a look of shock on their faces. NJC went on to explain that he wanted to bring about change and that the term 'Professional White Hunter' would change to 'Professional Hunter' and I would be the first to hold this title. I was to learn a great deal in a very short time.

It was at the end of the 2nd World War when NJC joined ranks with Peter Hankin. Norman would run the tourist facilities, whilst Peter would do hunting safaris. I learned a great deal from both these men. My knowledge of the bush increased in leaps and bounds.

One of my duties was to go and meet the passengers arriving on a DC3 aircraft. I would stand at one end of the apron with my arms in the air and guide the pilot to a parking spot. When I clapped my hands together the pilot would stop. After disembarking, the pilot would tell me to offload the luggage from the compartment marked MFE. When the luggage was identified, I would take the guests to Mfuwe, leaving NJC to clear the aircraft, wait for its departure and follow us to Mfuwe camp.

On arrival, the guests were shown to their rooms followed by a short game drive. As evening came, we settled down to a few beers and an opportunity to get to know each other. 9pm was lights out and at 5.30am tea and coffee was served on the main veranda. We'd set off on a game drive with my guarantees of seeing the big Five, plus all the other extras.

My programme for the first season was taking guests on the morning and evening drives. There were many satisfied clients. The day would end with beers and tall stories around a camp fire.

I will always remember my first game drive. Mwenda, the game guard, sat in the front seat next to me holding his 458 rifle confidently. We had six visitors with their cameras and binoculars and Norman Carr was there to see us off. At about 6am the mist was rising from the Luangwa River when Mwenda ordered me to stop. Elephants were crossing the river. It was a beautiful site. The biggest herd I have ever seen crossing the river was a herd of eighty elephants at Mwombosa wa Kumba.

In October 1971, I began my first season doing walking safaris. These were known as 'Wilderness Trails'. Throughout east and southern Africa, all hunting and guiding was being done by White Professional Hunters. This mould was broken when I started as an assistant guide in 1968 for Luangwa Safaris.

Mid October is very hot in the valley and it was late afternoon when we came across a group of six elephants consisting of female and young. Mwenda, the armed scout led us cautiously toward this group. My clients that day were a family of three from the Copperbelt. I had explained to them that in the event of a serious charge, they were to rally behind me whilst Mwenda would hold his fire until the very last minute. When, at ten metres, the elephant didn't seem like slowing down, I ordered Mwenda to shoot. There was a loud bang and she fell in her tracks. All the other elephants milled around her and that allowed us to get as far away from the scene as quickly as possible. It was a sad occasion, but the safety of my clients was paramount and I had to make a decision.

The Game Department accepted our explanations and with our clients as witnesses there was no case to answer.

Chibembe was the headquarters for 'Wilderness Trails'. The first trail leaders were Doug Skinner, Tony Moore, David Llyod, Dan Gough, Johnnie Roxborough and myself. We had a good working relationship and Norman Carr's family took me in as a family member. I got on well with Judy, Pam and Adrian.

My best memories were working at Chibembe. The Walking Safaris were for five nights out camping. We walked in single file. The armed scout ahead, me second, the clients next and the tea bearers brought up the rear. The Luangwa never failed to please both mammal and bird lovers.

One close encounter was in an area called Zebra Flats. Lions blend in well with the sandy soil and brown grass and before we knew it, all hell had broken loose. Two big males, four females and eight sub-adult cubs came at us. I shouted at the scout to fire. Three deafening shots rang out of his 375 H&H rifle. The shots frightened the lions, which turned and fled. Our hearts racing, we were unable to say anything for a while, maybe a little unintelligible garble.

The Luangwa has two seasons, rainy and dry. The dry season was for tourists, so we spent the rainy season fixing what needed fixed and preparing for the next dry season.

Some of our walking safaris took us waist-deep crossing the Luangwa River.

I would lead, then the clients and then an armed guard, followed by nine camp staff with provisions on their heads. The noise we made crossing the river frightened the crocodiles and hippos.

Some of our trips took us into the North Luangwa. This was real virgin territory- Africa at its wildest. We usually camped in four different spots along the clear, shallow, flowing rivers. Camping under the large wild fig trees in the full moon, sipping luke warm beers. Well……, we watched the stars in awe. Could I ever forget this?……..No.

Chapter Five

The Rainy Season

The rainy season ushers in a completely different dimension. The colours change very quickly. The leaves turn all shades of green, the flowers bloom from seeds that lay dormant during the dry season, and the butterflies with their vivid colours are much more evident against the lush green backdrop.

I visit the Luangwa with totally different expectations. I know that my movement within the park will be restricted as there is an abundance of water everywhere, and I can only use the all weather gravel road in the Mfuwe area. The rains have brought the temperature down a little even though there is higher humidity.

The vivid colours of the insect life which no artist can replicate, the abundant ant life and other crawling insects all showing a new sense of life, carrying their booty from one hole to the next. Don't get me wrong, all the other animals are still around, and we occasionally get interrupted by elephants or even lion sitting on the roads because they don't like the wet grass.

Gordon Trindade nicknamed me Butterfly Dundee as I pursued these elusive creatures with my camera. Keennan wasn't any help either, he thought it was very funny. Sometimes Keennan would ask if that butterfly was really that important, as he pointed to fresh lion spoor leading into the same long grass where the butterfly went.

I have found that no season is the wrong one for me, there is always something to appreciate. Even watching the build up of a genuine African thunderstorm, the distant thunder and lightning, definitely creation cries of the one who speaks in the thunder!

Thunderstorm

Potholes

Even though much work has been done to try and create all weather roads, there are always softer areas that will slowly give way, until there is a great big hole by the end of the rainy season. The lodges are all kitted out with four wheel drive vehicles, and will get you around without any problems.

The rains have washed away all the dust, and allowed the full colour of the African bush to come to the fore. Crocodiles roam far and wide enjoying the comfort of the still waters over the swift flowing Luangwa. A reminder to take care when approaching all flood plains.

Thunderstorm over Luangwa Wafwa

The scene above is the dry season version of the opposite page. Accessibility is much easier during the dry season, though each season has it's own specialities.

The butterflies are spectacular

David ~ Kelly

Egrets

Crocodiles

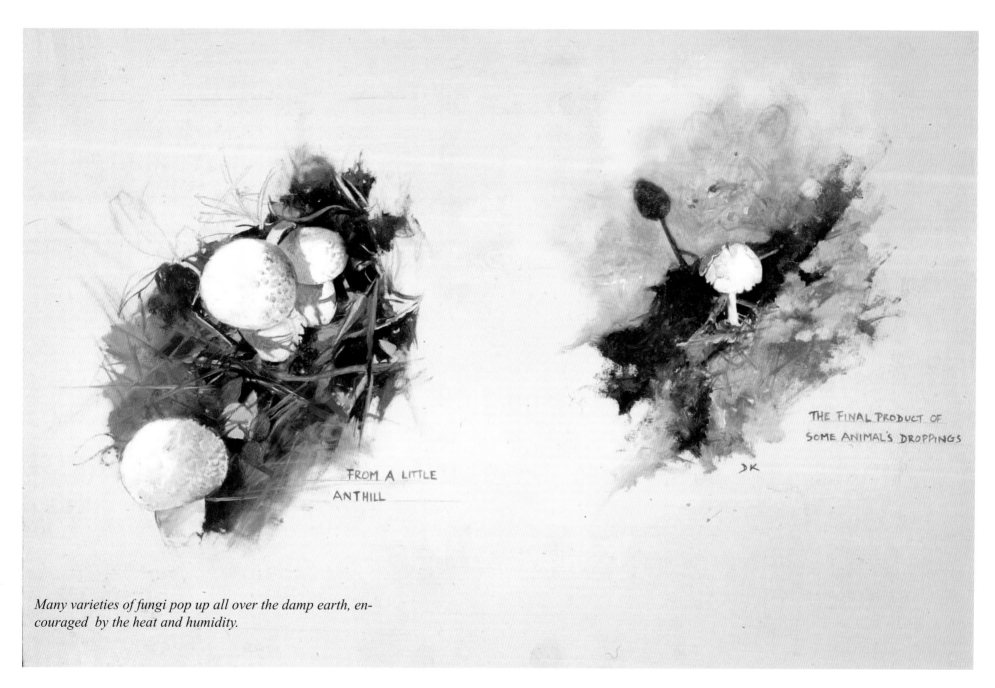

FROM A LITTLE
ANTHILL

THE FINAL PRODUCT OF
SOME ANIMAL'S DROPPINGS

DK

Many varieties of fungi pop up all over the damp earth, encouraged by the heat and humidity.

Unlike most other animals, the Wild dog seemed quite comfortable with our presence. As long as I kept low, their curiosity would heighten, and they really came up close. As they approached their heads would be lowered and their eyes fixed on me.

Right- *African Wild Dog*

David – Kelly

64

Left- *Butterfly*

My interest in all creatures great and small has increased dramatically since my move to Scotland. When I am back in Africa almost everything that moves grabs my attention, including tse tse flies and mosquitoes, which I give a different kind of attention.

Left - *Ipomoea*

Young impala

65

David-Kelly

A CLOSE ENCOUNTER WITH A LIONESS
Philip Berry

It is inevitable that when one is frequently in close proximity to dangerous animals there are sometimes exciting moments. Perhaps my most nerve-wracking was in 1963 when I introduced Tony Goddard, a friend who was a District Officer in the Provincial Adminis-tration, to his first wild lion.

The two of us were walking up the broad sandy bed of the Munina River in the Chilongozi sector of the South Luangwa Game Reserve (as it was then called) looking for a pair of lions that had been resident there for some days. Spotting two tiny lion cubs peering through a gap in a Combretum bush on the riverbank fifty metres away, I pointed them out to my colleague. The presence of the cubs presented a potentially dan-gerous situation and I was anxious for Tony to have a quick look and then we would retreat to a safer distance before an irate lioness appeared on the scene. However,

Tony had difficulty in seeing the cubs, and then it was too late. Without warning, two lionesses burst out of the same Combretum bush, one racing away upstream whilst the other charged straight towards us giving continuous snarling grunts. I shall never forget the sight of that lioness in full charge as her paws sent the sand flying up behind her. Fortunately the loose deep sand impeded her speed; otherwise she would have reached us much sooner. Nevertheless, she seemed to be cover-ing those fifty metres at an impressive rate!

I now fired a shot from my Jeffrey .404 rifle into the sand in front of the lioness, which had the welcome effect of causing her to slide to a halt a several paces from me. She lay there, crouched flat, growling fero-ciously up at me, and thumping her tail furiously from side to side on the sand. Meanwhile, I had automati-cally ejected the spent cartridge case from the rifle and slid another round forward from the magazine. To my dismay the cartridge jammed in the breech. As I found later, the leading edge of the casing had crumpled which caused it to become tightly jammed. Despite my frantic efforts with the bolt, the cartridge could not be ejected. For what seemed an interminable time, but was probably only a minute or so, the three of us were frozen in place me holding a useless rifle, the lioness crouched and extremely angry, and, hopefully, Tony Goddard still standing behind me, though I could not turn to look. Finally to my immense relief, the lioness rose and bounded away, back to where her cubs were hidden, feeling no doubt that she had made her point. I was now able to turn around and found Tony still standing there, somewhat shaken, but very impressed by his first encounter with a wild lion! As for me, I had no immediate reaction to the incident. It was only later, when back at my Lusangazi Camp that I developed a delayed but intense attack of the shakes, which lasted for a lengthy period!

Left top- *Wild Jasmin*

67

Hibiscus

Adult male Puku

Left - *Wildebeest on the run*

This tree's root system could not cope with the water saturation and erosion, and has fallen.

This white throated monitor lizard came out of the long green and wet grass onto the road in front of us and stopped. He was in no hurry to move on, and seemed to be enjoying the warm road surface.

WHITE THROATED MONITOR LIZARD

71

Malachite Kingfisher

The Malachite Kingfisher is a jewel of the African waterways. Found mainly close to water, it perches on low branches or reeds waitng to pounce on it's prey.

The rainy season roads are usually quite bad, and some areas have quite deep trenches. This Blacksmith Plover walks over to the trench in a bid to satisfy it's curiosity.

Mushilashi River

AN ELEPHANT SCARE
Philip Berry

In 1979, 1 was driving back to Mfuwe with Patrick Ansell and several wildlife scouts in a topless Land Rover that was quite ancient and mechanically impaired. If it was driven at less than about 30 kilometres an hour, the engine stalled, so one had to keep going and hope that nothing got in the way. We were just rounding a thicket where the road hugged the edge of the high bank of the Luangwa River. There was a single Combretum bush clinging to the bank edge, which seemed barely big enough to conceal a small animal. Nevertheless, to our horror, an adult cow elephant rushed out from behind this very bush and into the road in front of us. Despite the suddenness of her appearance, I was still trying to maintain the necessary speed to avoid stalling. By now elephant and Land Rover were moving in tandem, at one point the cow's left flank looming beside me so that I could have reached out and touched her. Fortunately she was as terrified as we were. Trumpeting in fright, she continued running and though at one point her flank bashed against the vehicle in front of my door she did not turn to attack it.

In trying to avoid hitting her again, I had to swing the vehicle to the left and reduce speed. The Land Rover promptly stalled and rolled to a halt. Sitting in stunned silence, we expected the elephant at any moment to stop and spin around and unleash the full extent of her fury upon us. Thankfully, she kept on screaming and running. I looked around at my companions, all of whom were in a state of shock. I wondered whether it was my imagination that the scouts huddled in the back of the vehicle seemed to have a distinctly lighter complexion than usual!

Having experienced a mock charge that morning, I wondered whether this elephant had adopted a new way of making us feel unwelcome

Chapter Six

Michael Ronaldson

I was born in February 1927 at Blantyre Mission hospital in Nyasaland which was a British protectorate. My father was Irish and my mother African. After working with Mulanje Mountain forestry project, I heard of a vacancy with the Game Department in Northern Rhodesia as Zambia was known then. I met a Major Taylor, who interviewed me. After satisfying his criteria, I was issued with basic supplies including a tent and a weapon, and sent on my way to the Luangwa Game Reserve as it was known then. This was a time of great racial prejudice and suspicion. Being of mixed race gave me the advantage of being able to identify with both cultures and therefore I was a sort of bridge between the Europeans and the Zambians. As a boss, Major Taylor allowed me to use my initiative and prove my ability to work independently.

My first big project was to construct a road down the Muchinga Escarpment. I had done some rock blasting on the Mulanje Mountain and was able to get on with clearing the road area. My ability to survey and calculate gradients using a Theodolite proved invaluable. I was then left to carry out the work alone with a team of motivated Zambians. I built a very nice bush camp half way down the escarpment which my immediate boss Lyndsay Birch aptly named Ronaldson's Camp. I don`t know how many times he shook my hand congratulating me for work well done. All this led to my early promotion to Game Ranger, and all the perks that went with it.

The Bridge on the Lupande River.

During the election year of 1963 I was asked to remain at Mfuwe during the rains to monitor the water levels. I told Captain Bullock that I would only be able to do that if I had access over the Lupande in case I needed to get any of my family out in an emergency. He asked if I had any proposals, so I put together some sketches of a proposed suspension bridge, with an estimate of cost as well. Captain Bullock showed the diagrams to the provincial road engineer, who discarded them to the bottom of his files as madness. The then Provincial Commissioner, Mr. Goodfellow said he had heard that I had suggestions of building a suspension bridge and had asked what had happened? Captain Bullock told him that Mr. Walker the engineer, thought that the plan was nonsense, and the cost of £800 too much. Mr. Goodfellow felt that as it was election year nothing should hinder the movement of ballot boxes so he gave the £800 for the construction. I built the bridge, and did five test runs myself, before radioing Captain Bullock advising him of completion. The project ended up costing £600 and taking only two and a half weeks. Captain Bullock came down on the Saturday afternoon and we met at the bridge. I then had to demonstrate it`s saftey again by driving over it four or five times. We shook hands then went to the camp for further discussions. He left late in the afternoon for Fort Jamieson, now Chipata, and reported the bridge's completion to Mr. Goodfellow.
The Provincial engineer was not happy as he insisted that I had broken the law with the bridge's location. His murmurings meant taking the bridge down and relocating it. The villagers were angry. They wanted to meet this Mr. Walker to find out why he was taking away their only means of access. I knew it would get nasty, so after much pacification and a promise to reconstruct, the pressure dropped. Unfortunately the rains started, so the next bridge was put up hastily and with much difficulty. After a while I could not guarantee it`s safety.

Story about Black Mamba.

I had gone up to Lion Camp for a few days to do some work. Being a Ranger meant travelling around the park and sometimes staying away from base camp for a few days. When we got there I erected my tent, and got on with my official duties. The day was very hot and I knew that there would be very little respite from the heat at night. The night sky was well lit with the three-quarter moon, so I had left my tent flaps open to try and get whatever breeze was blowing. With my rifle by my side, I fell into a light sleep.
I couldn`t have been asleep for more than an hour and a half, when I was awakened with a strange sound of movement. I looked out towards the scout camp, and my eyes dropped to ground level. There was a long dark snake making it`s rapid entry into my tent. It`s back shone with the moon's reflection. I froze and closed my eyes, opening them again just as suddenly but I saw no snake. Shakily I turned on my camp bed to look at the other side. I breathed a sigh of relief as I saw the snake's rear end disappear through the tall grass. My tent was no obstacle to it and as long as it did not see me I was no threat. My body temperature must have dropped a little as I felt a little cooler for a while.
I did not see that many snakes when I worked in the Luangwa, and I thought that the flooding during the rainy season might have had something to do with that. I had many more encounters with snakes when I worked in the Kafue Game Reserve.

Fishing.

My reputation as a fisherman had Johnny Uys our Warden recommending my services to any high profile visitors who wanted to go fishing. The former President of Zambia, Dr. Kenneth Kaunda, wanted to catch some fish. I soon realised that he had no idea how to fish, so I patiently taught him. We ended the day with quite a few bream. There was always preparation for my fishing forays, and I preferred a day's advance warning so that I would throw maize bran in the water to invite more fish into the area.

The then Governor General of Rhodesia and Nyasaland, Lord Dalhousie, was another of my fishing clients. The day before I took him fishing, I killed a chicken for my lunch and evening meal and hung the intestines in the fork of a tree to putrify. By the next day they had made very good bait for the giant catfish known as Vundu. We got onto the pontoon and fished mid-stream. It was a very successful day. Lord Dalhousie landed a forty-eight pounder after forty-five minute battle.

My Wart hog

I had gone up towards Big Lagoon game viewing and patrolling with my driver Penyani Banda. As we drove we came upon two very young warthogs by themselves. Surveying the whole area revealed no sign of their parents, so I told Penyani to choose which one he would pursue. Left alone they would soon fall prey to some carnivore or raptor. We took off at high speed, each pursuing his own quarry. Fortunately, mine ran down a river bank into the exposed roots of a fallen tree. It was cornered and it`s only escape was straight at me. I caught mine and went back to the car to find Penyani tongue out, panting heavily, having had no success. He tried explaining in between pants but I dismissed it knowing full well at what speed warthogs can run. I did not realise what I`d let myself in for. Having adopted me as it`s parent the warthog followed me everywhere. If I wanted to get away I used to have to leave it some dirty clothing, or my boots, and it would put it's snout in the boot and go to sleep.

When it had grown it started becoming a bit of a nuisance. It would knock over cooking pots, and eat the contents, including meat. Norman Carr once had a male warthog, which when he was closing Mfuwe Tourist camp he had given to Vivian Wilson, so I decided to give my adopted warthog to Vivian, also.

Elephant Rescue.

I was on vehicle patrol with some scouts and as we crossed a dried out riverbed we noticed a flexible object swinging to and fro at a distance on the river bed. I told the driver to stop, we got off the vehicle, made sure our rifles were ready on safety, and cautiously walked towards the object. From a distance of about fifty metres we identified the object as the tip of an elephant's trunk coming up from the ground. I signalled for us to spread out a little and we made our approach. The elephant and calf had walked on some kind of quicksand, and their desperate attempts to get out had only caused them to sink deeper. Both animals were very distressed by now. The calf was not too deep for us to attempt a rescue. As we dug, we too were sinking, so the operation took a whole day. We finally managed to drag the calf with six-inch tusks to temporary safety. Using the Half Linger, we carried it to Mushroom, where I was staying. We radioed the vet in Fort Jamieson, who said he`d come the following day. We tried to build up the calf's strength with water and leaves, but unfortunately it died that night. I did have some success with rescuing other animals, although we were not really kitted out for that sort of work.

Chapter Seven

Nsefu Sector

I visited the Nsefu Sector with Gerard Grant
(a friend) and Duncan, one of Mfuwe Lodges
guides.

*At full gallop this male Kudu with several females were trying
to distance themselves from us.*

Left- *This near barren landscape with a few broken mopane trees and sparse grassland had been recently burnt.*

Right-*The mineral rich saltpans support lush vegetation, and a variety of wildlife. These cranes are part of a variety of birds we saw in the area.*

79

Three impala on the salt plains.

Right- *Leopard Tortoise*

Left- *The trees are very spread out around the salt pan.*

Right- *Tails in the air, this family of warthog were leaving the saltpans for the thicker forest area. There was evidence around of predators, as we saw the remains of buffalo and impala.*

81

Hotspring

A creeper gone mad

83

Tafika Camp

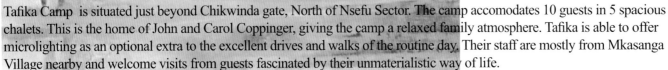

Tafika Camp is situated just beyond Chikwinda gate, North of Nsefu Sector. The camp accomodates 10 guests in 5 spacious chalets. This is the home of John and Carol Coppinger, giving the camp a relaxed family atmosphere. Tafika is able to offer microlighting as an optional extra to the excellent drives and walks of the routine day. Their staff are mostly from Mkasanga Village nearby and welcome visits from guests fascinated by their unmaterialistic way of life.
During the rainy season they offer river safaris with boating and canoeing. Exceptional bird watching and breathtaking scenes of the Luangwa in full flood are what you will see on these safaris.

Nsefu is the oldest tourist camp in the South Luangwa. The lodge is owned by Robin Pope Safaris. The scenery is stunning, and the accomodation comfortable. It is a seasonal camp, as access in the rainy season is impossible. Jason was the manager when I visited, and he was both helpful and very pleasant.

Jason , the manager at Nsefu lodge told me to look out for this
Wild fig tree with it's unusual trunk and root system.

Lilac breasted roller

We stopped for a break under some trees, when I noticed what looked like hollow clay balls. They all had a hole and there was a noticeable smell of the dung beetle. There was a hole in the earth near by, and Duncan said that the Honey Badger was responsible. It is able to pick up the scent through the cracks in the soil, and then digs out these clay balls and feasts on the Dung Beetle. So much for being called a Honey Badger.

Dung beetle rolling a ball of dung

Crocodile river

Termite mound

THE INEVITABLE END
NO CEREMONIES

We met Daudi Njobvu at Tena Tena. The camp is owned by Robin Pope Safaris, and Daudi is the manager. It was very refreshing to see a camp run by a Zambian national. He was both pleasant and professional, and we felt at ease. Daudi showed us around the camp and the stunning river scene. There was a tame family of warthog grazing under the trees.

Tena Tena

LILAC BREASTED ROLLER

Nsefu Sector

DAUD — LODGE MANAGER

Baka Baka Lagoon

LUNGA LAGOON

KAULUZI R.

Tena Tena camp

Luangwa RIVER

Milyoti Gate

89

View from Tena Tena

As we left the Nsefu sector of the park, I couldn't help feeling that I would be back one day. This vast land had so much to offer the wildlife enthusiast. The Nsefu sector is only accessible in the dry season, and it is advisable to use a four wheel drive vehicle as you have to cross a few sandy river beds.

The River

Mark Sprong

Luangwa is close to Lilongwe, and when the road is freshly graded the journey takes between three to four hours. Our proximity to Lilongwe was a major factor in the growth of our business since 1989. Our first safari vehicle was a 1965 forward control Land rover. Our mechanic drove, which was necessary, as the main Chipata to Mfuwe access road was terrible. Tie rod ends broke, gearboxes faltered, springs snapped, and fuel tanks developed holes in the most remote places.

We ran our first exploratory trip in 1989 and thereafter called ourselves, Land and Lake Safari. As a South African, I was not allowed into Zambia till 1992/3 due to apartheid. My first memory of Zambian officialdom is being treated with cynicism. I still recall being in Chipata and walking down an office corridor piled high on both sides with, one imagines, rejected entry requests. Only after numerous visits was I able to convince Zambian officialdom that my intentions were genuine and beneficial. My wife Angela operated the first tours with predominantly Dutch clients. Being British, Angela did not need a visa.

James and Annette Schulz were our hosts in the Luangwa. Annette was the driving force, and James was always mid-project. The best night drives were when James drove and Annette spotted. Once we saw 13 leopard in 3 days! Chilembo their cook, decked out in decrepit string vest, produced the most excellent meals from a bush stove with one plate working. Late at night we would hear the most dreadful racket and it transpired that James' staff were banging pots and pans together furiously, in a vain attempt to chase the elephants away from their kitchen garden. This was generally futile and we would know it was not working when James reverted to firing shots over the elephants heads, hoping to chase them away. The Schulz house was a two-storey affair and one wet season this turned out to be just as well as the Luangwa River flooded its banks and their house. They were forced to move all their belongings upstairs and camp.

Game drives always produce happy clients with game sightings unsurpassed. There are times in every operator's life when the guests are more entertaining than the animals they are supposed to be watching. Topless girls on the vehicle roof rack attracted many grins and strange looks from other tour operators. Acacia thorns can shred shirts from unsuspecting bodies. The times guests have climbed out of a vehicle, and dropped camera or binocular lenses in the close proximity of dangerous animals.

I once had the most eventful drive from Mfuwe to Petauke. I had a puncture

91

'Is it far?' *It took me a full day to drive it. Walking? Well if you follow the meander you could walk for months.*
'Is there water?' *Not a drop in October other than in the Luangwa River, except for the occasional unpalatable mineral spring.*
'What is the best way?' *Frankly I would now fly over this area.*

Asking for directions in the bush can produce the most confusing results. 'Just go to such and such a tree and clearly in front of you is a track or cut line which you cannot miss and follow this straight to the river / scout camp.' It's easy to miss entire areas let alone obscure cut lines possibly last cleared 5 years before. In all my years I have never come across a straight road and there are always tracks leading off created for one reason or another.

The Luangwa valley is unique and quite by far the most stunning and endearing game sanctuary in the region.

and repaired it, had another puncture and repaired that one too. Then I broke my pump and had another puncture, so I walked for one hour to a village and found a man with a motorbike. I was kindly given the use of this to hunt down another suspect pump, which I used to repair now two damaged tyres. Finally I followed what was sometimes a walking trail to arrive at Petauke at dusk.

We've done a lot to promote the area, and are asked questions by guests from the most basic 'Will we see animals?' to the rather more bizarre, 'we want to walk from Mfuwe to Petauke. Can we do this and will we find water en route?' (It was October).
Two adventurers wanted to walk this route and asked: -
'Is it easy?' *I battled to drive it.*
'Is it safe?' *There are wild animals, no water, no people and no facilities. No it's not safe.*

Chapter 8
Lodges along the river

There are a number of lodges situated outside the Park in the Game Management Area. They all have the Luangwa River at their front and you can enjoy the view as well as the hospitality they provide.

Marula Lodge

I have stayed at Marula on three occasions. The price is right and you are accommodated in comfortable two bed roomed chalets that have fans and hot water. The price includes breakfast, and they can supply other basic meals. The staff are friendly and they provide game activities in the form of game drives, both day and night.

Flatdogs

Flatdogs

If you are looking to meet a lot of people and want to combine your safari experience with socializing, Flatdogs is the place. They offer budget accommodation and have self-catering facilities. They have a camping area and can accommodate overland trucks. I have not stayed there myself, but Graeme Cranko, a friend, raves about the place. They also offer game drives.

Kapani

Kapani Lodge

Kapani Lodge is owned by Norman Carr Safaris and has a very good reputation. They probably, more than any other lodge, have to be on their toes, because of the late Norman Carr's legacy. They offer game drives and walking safaris, and run various seasonal bush camps.

Nkwali

Nkwali is the headquarters of Robin Pope Safaris. The lodge is comfortable and the service good. I met Simon Cousins, an employee of Robin Pope Safaris. He was very friendly and helpful.

Simon Cousins   Nkwali

Wildlife Camp

Wildlife Camp is owned and run by Herman Miles. They have comfortable budget accommodation, and will prepare food on request. They have camping facilities and can accommodate overland trucks. They also offer game drives.

Kafunta Riverside Lodge

Kafunta is owned and run by Ron and Anke, both very friendly and accommodating. Their place is both comfortable and very scenic. They offer both day and night drives, and walking safaris. They also have a bush camp.

Kafunta

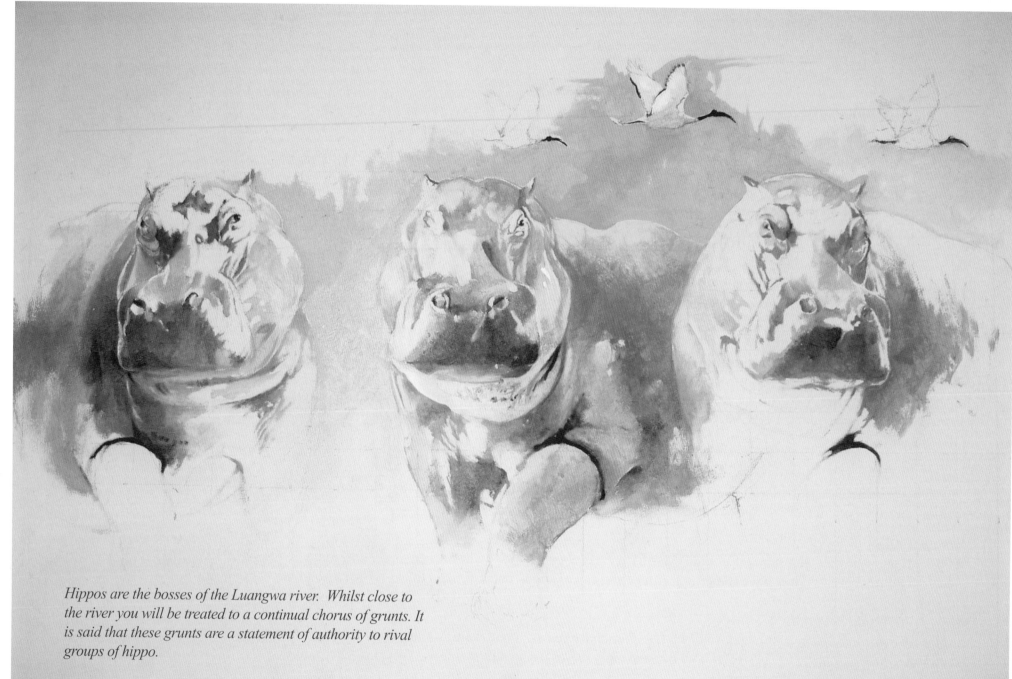

Hippos are the bosses of the Luangwa river. Whilst close to the river you will be treated to a continual chorus of grunts. It is said that these grunts are a statement of authority to rival groups of hippo.

Zebra

Left - The Barn owl is nocturnal, and it's shrieks can be heard at night. It feasts mainly on rodents. It is a very beautiful bird and can be found in the Northern hemisphere..

95

R.A.T.S.

R.A.T.S. stands for Rapid Action Teams and they undertake patrols to combat commercial poaching and transport of animal products, as well as the apprehension and prosecution of poachers. They were formed in 1997 by the lodges and operators of the South Luangwa National Park (SLNP) in response to increased poaching and in support of the work carried by Zambian National Parks and Wildlife (now known as ZAWA).

The SLNP and surrounding Game Management Areas (GMAs) are home to an abundance of wildlife and ecosystems as well as a population of around 50,000 people. The area has been exposed to commercial poaching for some considerable time. So far, the black rhino have been poached to extinction (in the early 1990s) and the elephant populations have been reduced from around 100,000 in the early 1970s to 5000 – 6000 in 2003 (South Luangwa Area Management Unit Census 2002).

RATS were set up to combat the high levels of poaching and to assist and strengthen ZAWA's over-stretched anti-poaching units. SLNP is one of the few wildlife areas left unspoiled by mass tourism. Mass tourism, however, does ensure low levels of poaching due to a large presence of tourists throughout the year. South Luangwa is unique in its success with relatively low tourist numbers, but this means that the wildlife is threatened by a higher, and year round level of poacher activity.

RATS consists of 16 dedicated local Zambians who are mostly ex Wildlife Officers or ex army personnel. They undertake short patrols of 1 – 2 days and long patrols to more remote areas of 5 – 10 days with 5 –7 officers and a ZAWA armed escort forming the patrol group. Over the years RATS have proved to be a valuable and successful in maintaining an anti-poaching presence and gaining some significant successes with arrests of poachers, ivory seizures and cross-border co-operation with the Malawi Anti-Corruption Bureau and Wildlife Department in uncovering a large ivory cartel operating out of Mfuwe, Chipata and Lilongwe.

They urgently enquire funding and donations of equipment to enable them to continue to carry out this vital role for the preservation of wildlife in and around the South Luangwa National Park.

All donations are gratefully received and go directly towards stopping poaching. All administration costs are voluntarily donated.

Tree beside the Mushilashi

David-Kelly

Left - I am still not sure about the identity of this lesser eagle. I managed to get up quite close for a shot, and left wondering whether it was a Tawny or Whalbergs eagle. Keennan said that it was a Whalbergs, so I have taken his expert word for it. Feel free to dispute the identification.

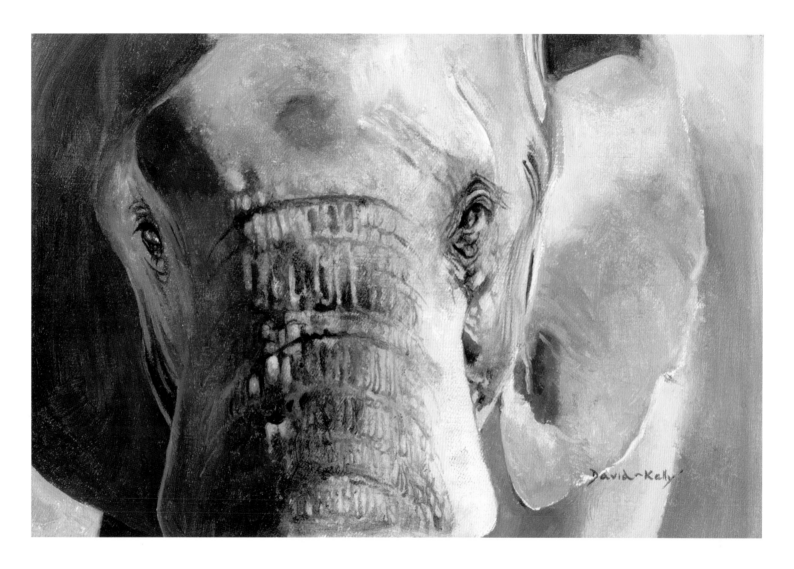

There is an abundance of animals to see in the Luangwa, and definitely no shortage of elephant. The elephant are quite familiar with tour vehicles, and will often allow you to come up quite close. You still have to be cautios, and being sensible will avoid any disasters. The experienced safari guides know and understand animal behaviour, and will guide you accordingly.

It is difficult for me to describe the exitement I feel when I come across a magnificent male lion. The title of King immediately springs to mind. This male seen drinking by Andy Hogg, did not stop what it was doing but satisfied it's thirst, looked around and then made for the shade of a tree. Animals spend the hotter parts of the day in the shade.

David-Kelly'

99

Chris Badger

Wilderness Safaris started their operation in Malawi in 1987 and also have quality properties in Botswana, Namibia, Zimbabwe and South Africa. They have a busy travel office in Lilongwe, run mobile safaris throughout the region and run Mvuu lodge and camp in Liwonde National Park, and Chintheche Inn on the Northern Shores of Lake Malawi.

'I was once staying at Nkwali Camp with a group of 8 guests. In those days we drove large 4-wheel drive Chevrolets that looked exactly like the ex-military vehicles they were. Going out for an evening drive on the narrow track that runs from Nkwali to the park gate, we rounded a corner, perhaps a little too quickly and narrowly missed colliding with an open safari vehicle coming towards us. The vehicle had two passengers. One passenger had a look of almost mystic calm, and the other looked horrified. The calm one was Norman Carr, doyen of all the Luangwa guides and founder of Kapani Safari Lodge. The guest who may have seen his life flash before him was the Duke of Edinburgh.'

Wilderness Safaris

Chapter Nine
To Chamilandu

The trip to Chamilandu will take you anything up to three hours. Certain portions of the road are alright, but where you find the ungraded black cotton soil it feels like riding on rocks. Guests are usually taken on the alternative route outside the park which takes them to a pontoon crossing quite close to the bush camps..

Above - Flower from the sausage tree

The Woodland kingfisher is a very beautiful bird that is seen mainly in the rainy season. It's bright blue colours flash across the landscape as it flies around. It also has a loud call.

Woodland Kingfisher

Male Puku

Female Bushbuck

Above - *I wonder just how many Guinea fowl are in the South Luangwa. Everywhere you go it does not take time to see a flock of anything up to fifty birds. On this trip I found that a baboon had killed a Guinea fowl, and was being pursued by quite a few other baboons who wanted some of the booty.*

The colours on these elephant changed as the different soils and sand stuck to their wet skins. The elephant cake their bodies with mud to prevent biting insects from getting through.

Above - This cub was not alone when I took this picture. There was another cub just leaving to join the rest of the family seated about fifty metres away under a shady tree. As a painter I can change the composition at will.

Puku ridge

Chichele Lodge

Left - Chichele Lodge is situated on a hill that overlooks the Luangwa river on the left, and the Southern plains including the Chindeni hills. The lodge is owned by Star of Africa and is run by Mark Rashid. I met Mark for the first time when he was supervising the construction. The lodge is very nice and offers a luxurious, less rustic stay.

Left - This fallen tree trunk was quite old. With it's sun bleached look, I felt it made an interesting subject to paint. The red soil at it's base was part of a termite mound, that had made it's base here. I could only imagine how many little life forms were in existance in and around this tree.

Right - The palm forest on the right adds another dimension to the varied landscape and vegetation. I have seen plenty buffalo here, but also experienced the wrath of the Tsetse fly. This forest lies a few kilometres from the Manzi river.

Above - This buffalo had a rather gentle expression on his face, unlike the mean looking old bulls that glare at you with disdain. Buffalo have been one of my favourite subjects to paint, especially the mean old fellows. I have always wanted my paintings to convey some kind of message, and I hope they have done so to date.

Buffalo in the palm forest

AFRICAN STAR-CHESTNUT
STERCULIA AFRICANA

The primary boarding school I went to was situated in an area that still had untouched forests, as much of the surrounding areas were owned by farmers and left as natural woodland. At that time I really did not appreciate the beauty of the trees and wildlife, I only knew that some of the trees and plants had quite nasty bits on them. The African Chestnut has a hairy powder in it's pods, and they become accessible when the pods are dry and start to open. Boarding school is a breeding ground for mischief, and some of the lads would carefully harvest the hairs and put them in classmates' clothing. You can understand why this beautiful tree did not carry the same sentiments when I was a lad.

Yellowbilled Hornbill

Above - This cub was one of a group of three that paid us very little attention as we drew up close. The reason being, mummy and two aunties were about twenty feet away watching our every move.

Manzi river

The banks of the Manzi river show layers of different types of rock and sand formations. The colours are very beautiful. The Manzi river only flows in the rains, and therefore allows access across it during the dry months. You will still require a four wheel drive vehicle. The camp on the right is called Kuyenda, which means walking. The camp is situated beside the Manzi river, and is expertly run by Phillip Berry and Babette Alfieri. The camp is owned by The Bushcamp Company. Phil's experience and knowledge will make your wild-life experience the best you are ever likely to get anywhere in Southern Africa. Whilst very comfortable, the design allows you to enjoy a real bush experience The service is excellent.

Babette Alfieri

Lilac breasted roller

The Lilac breasted roller is commonly seen throughout the park. It displays its very vivid and magnificent colours as it flies around. They always seem to fly alone, so in terms of numbers, there are probably not that many.

Chamilandu

The Bushcamp Company own and run Chamilandu camp. The camp is situated under huge mahogany trees that provide much needed shade. The view is very beautiful and the accomodation wonderful. The scene above is the view from the camp.

Right -   Chindeni is another of The Bushcamp Company's seasonal camps. Facing the river the view is magnificent. The accomodation and service exquisite. Your experience here will live with you for many years.

Right - Bilimungwe is the furthest of the camps owned and run by The Bushcamp Company. It also offers excellent accomodation, safari activities and a friendly service

Left - *Buffalo*

Keennan Thole

Keennan was born in Lusaka on the 12th of December 1965. He has worked in the South Luangwa for nineteen and a half years. He has now worked with Mfuwe Lodge for four and a half years and currently holds the position of a senior guide.

I met Keennan nearly two years ago, and have found him to be friendly, helpful, very knowledgeable, and confident. I can only compare him to an old friend of mine called Obedi Mkandawire, who works for the department of wildlife in Malawi. They both have a deep rooted interest in the preservation of wildlife, and have taken it upon themselves to learn as much as possible about the animals they work with.

I am also able to communicate with him in the vernacular, so our discussions go a lot deeper than normal.

One morning Gerard, Keennan and myself set out on a game drive. It had all been going smoothly, until the road came very close to the rivers edge. Three elephant were coming over the rise. It was a mother and two calves of varying ages. She immediately charged, and what does Keennan do ? He stalled the car "deliberately". I have never seen an angry elephant so close, and fortunately it veered a little left to avoid contact. I had been told that when an elephant lowers it's head it means business, and that is exactly what this one did. Gerard got fantastic video footage (he was fortunate his camera has an image stabiliser) Excitedly, I took a few rather shaky photographs. There was no change in the immediate odour, so I can confirm that we took the whole incident quite well.

Of course Keennan still insists he deliberately stalled the vehicle, and that the engine did not just cut off, as he desperately tried to get away. We are still good friends.

KUDU

Kudu are very graceful antelope. From an artists view point, I find them a favourite to paint. The females have no horns, whilst a fully grown male can have three full turns in his horns. They are quite wide-spread, but stay close to shrubs and low trees where they can browse.

David ~ Kelly

117

Bateleur Eagle

The Bateleur eagle is never far from sight. They are always seen soaring the skies, and are rarely seen perched anywhere. In fact I managed to get my sketching material from a Bateleur in captivity at a bird sanctuary in the UK. Unfortunately that Bateleur would never experience its intended playground, and the freedom of the African skies.

Another day, another sunset. Every day a different back drop, unfortunately we have to leave, but we will be back............someday.

APPENDIX I

A Mamals Checklist

CARNIVORES
Family: Dogs and Allies
•Side-striped Jackal (Canis adustus)
•Wild Dog (Lycaon pictus)

Family: Mustelids
•Clawless Otter (Aonyx capensis)
•Honey Badger/Ratel (Mellivora capensis)
•African Striped Weasel (Poecilogale albinucha)
•Cape Polecat/Striped PolecatlZorilla
(Ictonyx striatus)

Family: Genets and Civets
•African Civet (Civettictis civetta)
•Rusty-spotted Genet (Genetta rubignosa)

Family: Mongooses
•Selous' Mongoose/Meerkat (Paracynictis selonsi)
•Bushy-tailed Mongoose (Bdeogale crasstcauda)
•Large Grey Mongoose (Herpestes ichneumon)
•Slender Mongoose (Galerella sanguinea)
•Meller's Mongoose (Rhynchogale melleri)
•White-tailed Mongoose (Ichneumia albicauda)
•Marsh Mongoose (Atilax paludinosus)
•Banded Mongoose (Mungos mungo)
•Dwarf Mongoose (Helogale parvula)

Family: Hyaenas
•Spotted Hyaena (Crocuta crocuta)

Family: Cats
•Cheetah (Acinonyx jubatus)
•Leopard (Panthera pardus)
•Lion (Panthera leo)
•Caracal (Caracal caracal)
•Serval (Leptailurus serval)
•African Wild Cat (Felis silvestris)

EVEN-TOED UNGULATES
Family: Pigs
•Common Warthog (Phacochoerus africanus)
•Bushpig (Potamochoerus porcus)

Family: Hippopotamus
•Hippopotamus (Hippopotamus amphibius)

Family: Giraffes
•Thomicrofl's Giraffe (Giraffa camelopardalis thornicrofti)

Family: Antelopes and Buffaloes
•Cookson's Wildebeest (Connochaetes taurinus cooksoni)
•Lichtenstein's Hartebeest (Sigmoceros lichtensteinii)
•Common Duiker (Sylvicapra grimmia)
•Klipspringer (Oreotragus oreotragus)
•Oribi (Ourebia ourebt)
•Sharpe's Grysbok (Raphicerus sharpei)
•Impala (Aepyceros melampus)
•Roan Antelope (Hippotragus equinus)
•Sable Antelope (Hippotragus niger)
•Buffalo (Syncerus caffer)
•Bushbuck (Tragelaphus scrtptus)
•Kudu (Tragelaphus strepsiceros)
•Eland (Taurotragus oryx)
•Reedbuck (Redunca arundinum)
•Waterbuck (Kobus elhpsiprymnus)
•Puku (Kobus vardonii)

ODD-TOED UNGULATES
Family: Rhinoceroses
•Black Rhinoceros (Diceros bicornis) (possibly extinct)

Family: Horses
•Burchell's Zebra (Equus quagga crawshayi)

ELEPHANTS
Family: Elephants
•African Elephant (Loxodonta africana)

PRIMATES
Family: Galagos and Bushbabies
•Thick-Tailed Bushbaby (Otolemur crassicaudatus)
•Night Ape/Lesser Bushbaby (Galago moholi)

Family: Old World Monkeys
•Moloney's Monkey (Cercopithecus albogularis)
•Vervet Monkey (Cercopithecus aethiops)
•Yellow Baboon (Papio cynocephalus)

AARDVARKS
Family: Aardvarks
•Aardvark/Antbear (Orycteropus afer)

PANGOLINS
Family: Pangolins
•Pangolin (Phataginus temminckii)

DASSIES
Family: Dassies/Hyraxes
•Yellow-spotted Dassie (Heterohyrax brucei)
•Tree Dassie (Dendrohyrax arboreus)

RABBITS AND HARES
Family: Hares
•Scrub Hare (Lepus victoriae)

RODENTS
Family: ***Squirrels***
•Sun Squirrel *(Heliosciurus mutabilis)*
•Bush Squirrel *(Paraxerus cepapi)*
Family: ***African Flying Squirrels***
•*Anomalurus derbianus*

Family: ***Porcupines***
•Porcupine *(Hystrix africaeaustralis)*

Family: ***Cane Rats***
•Greater Cane Rat *(Thryonomys swinderianus)*

Family: ***Mole Rats***
•Common Mole Rat *(Crptomys hottentotus)* *

Family: ***Rats, Mice and Gerbils***
•Bushveld Gerbil *(Tatera leucogaster)*
•Giant Rat *(Cricetmys gamhianus)*
•Pouched Mouse *(Saccostomus campestris)*
•Fat Mouse *(Steatomys pratensis)*
•Krebs' Fat Mouse *(Steatomys krebsii)*
•Spiny Mouse *(Acomys spinosissimus)* *
•Grooved-Toothed Mouse *(Pelomys fallax)*
•Single-Striped Mouse *(Lemniscomys rosalia)*
•Woodland Mouse *(Grammomys dolichurus)*
•Pygmy Mouse *(Mus minutoides)*
•Multimanimate Mouse *(Mastomys natalensis)*
•*Praomys jacksoni*
•Tree Mouse *(Thallomys paedulcus)*
•Red Veld Rat *(Aethomys chrysophilus)*
•Namaqua Rock Mouse *(Aethomys namaquensis)*
•Black Rat *(Rattus rattus)*

Family: ***Dormice***
•Woodland Dormouse *(Graphiurus microtis)*
•*Graphiurus kelleni*

INSECTIVORES
Family: ***Shrews***
•Lesser Red Musk Shrew *(Crocidura hirta)*
•Tiny Musk Shrew *(Crocidura fuscoinurina)*
•Greater Grey-brown Musk Shrew *(Crocidura Iuna)* *
Family: ***Hedgehogs***
•Four-toed Hedgehog *(Atelerix albiventris)* *

ELEPHANT SHREWS
Family: ***Elephant Shrews***
•Four-toed Elephant Shrew *(Petrodromus tetradacty-lus)*
•Short-snouted Elephant Shrew *(Elephantulus brachyrhynchus)*

BATS
Family: ***Fruit bats***
•*Epomophorus minor*
•Peters' Epauletted Fruit Bat *(Epomophorus crypturus)*
•Egyptian Fruit Bat *(Rousettus egyptiacus)*

Family: ***Tomb Bats***
•Tomb Bat *(Taphozous mauritainus)*

Family: ***Slit-faced Bats***
•Large Slit-Faced Bat *(Nycteris grandis)*
•Common Slit-Faced Bat *(Nycteris thebaica)*
•Greater Slit-Faced ~at *(Nycteris macrotis)*

Family: ***False Vampire Bats***
•*Lavia frons* *

Family: ***Horseshoe Bats***
•Hildebrandt's Horseshoe Bat *(Rhinolophus hilderbrandt)*
•Ruppell's Horseshoe Bat *(Rhinolophus fumigatus)* *
•Geoffioy' s Horseshoe Bat *(Rhinolophus clivosus)*
•Lander's Horseshoe Bat *(Rhinolophus landeri)*

Family: ***Leaf-nosed Bats***
•Sundevall's Leaf-Nosed Bat *(Hipposideros caffer)*
•*Hipposideros ruber*

Family: ***Simple-nosed Bats***
•Schreiber's Long-Fingered Bat *(Miniopterus shreibersii)*
•Yellow House Bat *(Scotophilus dinganii)*
•*Scotophilus viridis*
•Long-tailed Serotine *Bat (Eptesicus hottentotus]* *
•Banana Bat *(Pipistrellus nanus)*
•Somali Serotine Bat *(Pipistrellus somalicus)*
•Schlieffen's Rat *(Nycticeinops schlieffenii)*
•*Scotoecus hirundo*
•Damara Woolly *(KerivouIa argentata)* *

Family: ***Mastiff Bats***
•Little Free-Tailed Bat *(Tadarida pumila)* *

APPENDIX II

A Birds Checklist

RAPTORS
Cuckoo Hawk *(African Cuckoo Hawk)*
Honey Buzzard
Bat Hawk
Blackshouldered Kite
Yellowbilled Kite
Black Kite
African Fish Eagle
Palmnut Vulture
Hooded Vulture
Whitebacked Vulture *(African White-backed Vulture)*
Lappetfaced Vulture
Whiteheaded Vulture
Rueppell's Vulture
Blackbreasted Snake Eagle *(Short-toed Eagle)*
Brown Snake Eagle
Western Banded Snake Eagle
Bateleur
Gynmogene
European Marsh Harrier
African Marsh Harrier
Pallid Harrier
Dark Chanting Goshawk
GabarGoshawk
Black Sparrowhawk *(Black Goshawk)*
Ovambo Sparrowhawk
Little Sparrowhawk
African Goshawk
Shikra
Lizzard Buzzard
Steppe Buzzard (Common Buzzard)

Augur Buzzard
Wahlberg's Eagle
Lesser Spotted Eagle
Greater Spotted Eagle
Tawny Eaglc
Steppe Eagle
African Hawk Eagle
Booted Eagle
Ayres's Hawk Eagle
Longcrested Eagle
Crowned Eagle
Martial Eagle
Osprey
Secretary Bird
Lesser Kestrel
Dickinson's Kestrel
Eastern Redfooted Kestrel *(Eastern Red-footed Falcon)*
Rednecked Falcon
Hobby Falcon *(European Hobby)*
Lanner Falcon
Peregrine Falcon

FOWLS
Coqui Francolin
Shelley's Francolin
Natal Francolin
Hildcbrandt's Francolin
Swainson's Francolin
RedneckedFrancolin
Harlequin Quail
Blue Quail
Crested Guineafowl
Helmeted Guineafowl
Kurrichanc Buttonquail

LARGE WATER BIRDS
Little Grebe

Reed Cormorant
Darter
White Pelican
Pinkbacked Pelican
Little Bittern
Dwarf Bittern
Blackcrowned Night Heron
Whitebacked Night Heron
Squacco Heron *(Common Squacco Heron)*
Madagascar Squacco Heron
Rufousbcllied Heron
CattleEgret
Grecnbacked Heron
Black Egret
Little Egret
Yellowbilled Egret
Great White Egret
Purple Heron
Grey Heron
Blackheaded Heron
Goliath Heron
Hamerkop
Yellowbilled Stork
Openbill Stork
Black Stork
Abdim's Stork
Woollynecked Stork
White Stork
Saddlebilled Stork
Marabou Stork
Sacred Ibis
Glossy Ibis
Hadeda Ibis *(Hadada)*
African Spoonbill
Greater Flamingo
Lesser Flamingo
Fulvous Whistling Duck

Whitefaced Whistling Duck
WhitebackedDuck
Egyptian Goose
Spurwinged Goose
Knobbilled Duck
Pygmy Goose *(African Pygmy Goose)*
Redbilled Teal
HottentotTeel
Garganey
Southern Pochard
African Finfoot
Wattled Crane
Crowned Crane *(Southern Crowned Crane)*

SMALLER WATERBIRDS
Redchested Flufftail
African Rail *(African Water Rail)*
Coin Crake
African Crake
Black Crake
Striped Crake
Purple Gallinule
Lesser Gallinule
Moorhen *(Common Moorhen)*
Lesser Moorhen
Redknobbed Coot

BUSTARDS
Denham's Bustard
Blackbellied Korhaan *(Black-bellied Bustard)*

WADERS & PLOVERS
African Jacana
Lesser Jacana
Painted Snipe
Blackwinged Stilt

Avocet
Water Dikkop
Spotted Dikkop
Threebanded Courser
Bronzewinged Courser
Temminck's Courser
Redwinged Prantincole *(Common Pratincole)*
Rock Pratincole
Ringed Plover
Kittlitz's Plover
Threebanded Plover
Whitefronted Plover *(White-fronted Sand Plover)*
Sand Plover *(Greater Sand Plover)*
Caspian Plover
Wattled Plover *(Senegal Wattled Plover)*
Whitecrowned Plover
Blacksmith Plover
Lesser Blackwinged Plover
Crowned Plover
Longtoed Plover
Ethiopian Snipe
Great Snipe
Blacktailed Godwit
Whimbrel
Curlew
Marsh Sandpiper
Greenshank
Green Sandpiper
Wood Sandpiper
Terek Sandpiper
Common Sandpiper
Turnstone
Sanderling
Little Stint
Curlew Sandpiper
Ruff

GULLS, TERNS & SKIMMERS
Lesser Blacktacked Gull
Greyheadcd Gull
Whiskered Tern
Whitewinged Black Tetn
African Skimmer

SANDGROUSE
Doublebanded Sandgrouse

PIGEONS & DOVES
Laughing Dove
African Mourning Dove
Cape Turtle Dove
RedeyedDove
Greenspotted Dove *(Emerald-spotted Wood Dove)*
Tambourine Dove
Namaqua Dove
Green Pigeon

PARROTS
Cape Parrot *(Brown-necked Parrot)*
Meyer's Parrot
Lilian's Lovebird

MOUSEBIRDS & TROGONS
Redfaced Mousebird
Narina Trogon

LOURIES (TURACOS)
Schalow's Lourie *(Schalow's Turaco)*
Purplecrested Lourie *(Purple-crested Turaco)*
Ross's Lourie *(Lady Ross's Turaco)*
GreyLourie

CUCKOOS & COUCALS
Great Spotted Cuckoo
Jacobin Cuckooo
Striped Crested Cuckoo
Thickbilled Cuckoo
Redchested Cuckoo
Black Cuckoo
European Grey Cuckoo
African Grey Cuckoo
Lesser Cuckoo
Barred Cuckoo *(Barred Long-tailed Cuckcuoo)*
Emerald Cuckoo
Klaaa's Cuckoo
Diederik Cuckoo *(Didric Cuckoo)*
Black Coucal *(African Black Coucal)*
Senegal Coucal
Burchell's Coucal

OWLS
Barn Owl
Grass Owl
African Scops Owl
White-faced Owl
Spotted Eagle Owl
Giant Eagle Owl
Pel's Fishing Owl
Pearl-spotted Owlet
Barred Owlet
Wood Owl
Marsh Owl

NIGHTJARS
Fierynecked Nightjar
Freckled Rock Nightjar
Mozambique Nightjar *(Gaboon Nightjar)*
Pennantwinged Nightjar

SWIFTS
Mottled Spinetail
Batlike Spinetail
Palm Swift *(African Palm Swift)*
Alpine Swift
European Swift
Little Swift
Horus Swift
Whiterumpcd Swift *(African White-rumped Swift)*

KINGFISHERS
Halfcollared Kingfisher
Malachite Kingfisher
Pygmy Kingfisher
Brownhooded Kingfisher *(Brown-headed Kingfisher)*
Greyhooded Kingfisher *(Chestnut-bellied Kingfisher)*
Woodland Kingfisher *(Senegal Kingfisher)*
Striped Kingfisher
Giant Kingfisher
Pied Kingfisher

BEE-EATERS
Little Bee-eater
Swallowtailed Bee-eater
Whitefronted Bee-eater
Olive Bee-eater *(Madagascar Bee-eater)*
Bluecheeked Bee-eater
European Bee-eater
Carmine Bee-eater *(Southern Carmine Bee-eater)*

ROLLERS & HOOPOES
European Roller

Lilacbreasted Roller
Rackettailcd Roller
Purple Roller
Broadbilled Roller
Redbilled Woodhoopoe
Scimitarbillcd Woodhoopoe
(Scimitarbill)
Hoopoe

HORNBILLS
Redbilled Hornbill
Crowned Hornbill
Palebilled Hornbill
Grey Hornbill *(African Grey Hornbill)*
Trumpeter Hornsbill
Ground Hornbill *(Southern Ground Hornbill)*

BARBETS & HONEYGUIDES
Yellowfronted Tinkerbird
Blackcollared Barbet
Black-backed Barbet
Crested Barbet
Sharpbillcd Honeyguide *(Brown-backed Honeyguide)*
Scalythroated Honeyguide *(Scaly-fronted Honeyguide)*
Greater Honeyguide
Lesser Honeyguide

WOODPECKERS
Bennett's Woodpecker
Goldentailed Woodpecker
Cardinal Woodpecker
Bearded Woodpecker
Olive Woodpecker
African Broadbill

PITTA
Angola Pitta *(African Pitta)*

LARKS
Flappet Lark
Dusky Lark
Redcapped Lark
Chcstnut-backed Finchlark
Chestnut-backed Sparrow-lark)

SWALLOWS & MARTINS
Black Saw-wing
Sand Martin *(European Sand Martin)*
Brownthroated Martin *(African Sand Martin)*
Banded Martin
Greyrumped Swallow
Mosque Swallow
Lesser Striped Swallow
Wiretailed Swallow
Whitethroated Swallow
European Swallow
House Martin

WAGTAILS, PIPITS & LONGCLAWS
Yellow Wagtail
Longtailed Wagtail *(Mountain Wagtail)*
African Pied Wagtail
Richard's Pipit
Buffy Pipit
Striped Pipit
Yellowthroated Longclaw

CUCKOO-SHRIKES
Black Cuckoo-shrike
Whitebreasted Cuckoo-shrike

BULBULS
Yellowbellied Greenbul
Terrestrial Bulbul
Blackeyed Bulbul *(Common Bulbul)*

CHATS, ROBINS & THRUSHES
Kurrichane Thrush
Thrush Nightingale
Heuglin's Robin
Natal Robin *(Red-capped Robin)*
Collared Palm Thrush
Bearded Robin *(Eastern Bearded Scrub Robin)*
Whitebrowed Robin *(Whitebrowed Scrub Robin)*
Stonechat
Capped Wheatear
Familiar Chat
Amot's Chat

WARBLERS, APALISES & CISTICOLAS
Moustached Warbler *(African Moustached Warbler)*
European Sedge Warbler *(Sedge Warbler)*
European Reed Warbler *(Reed Warbler)*
European Marsh Warbler *(Marsh Warbler)*
Great Reed Warbler
Icterine Warbler
Greencapped Eremomela

Burntnecked Eremomela
Yellowbellied Eremomela
Longbilled Crombec
Willow Warbler
Yellowbreasted Hyliota *(Yellow-bellied Hyliota)*
Mashona Hyliota *(Southern Hyliota)*
Garden Warblet
Common Whitethroat
Fantailcd Cisticola
Rattling Cisticola
Shortwinged Cisticola
Neddicky
Redfaccd Cisticola

Tawnyflanked Prinia
Redwinged Warbler
Yellowbreasted Apalis
Bleating Warbler *(Bleating Bush Warbler)*
Miombo Barred Warbler

FLYCATCHERS
Black Flycatcher *(Southern Black Flycatcher)*
Spotted Flycatcher
Dusky Flycatcher
Bluegrey Flycatcher *(Ashy Flycatcher)*
Fantailed Flycatcher *(Lead-coloured Flycatcher)*
Chinspot Batis
Wattle-eyed Flycatcher *(Black-throated Wattle-eye)*
Livingstone's Flycatcher
Paradise Flycatcher

BABBLERS, TITS, CREEPERS AND WHITE-EYES
Arrowmarked Babbler
Southern Black Tit
Grey Penduline Tit
Spotted Creeper
Yellow White-eye

SUNBIRDS
Red-and-blue Sunbird
Violetbacked Sunbird
Collared Sunbird
Black Sunbird *(Amethyst Sunbird)*
Scarletchested Sunbird
Yellowbellied Sunbird
Whitebellied Sunbird
Shelley's Sunbird
Purplebanded Sunbird
Coppery Sunbird

ORIOLES & SHRIKES
European Golden Oriole
African Golden Oriole
Blackheaded Oriole *(Eastern Black-headed Oriole)*
Redbacked Shzike
Lesser Grey Shrike
Fiscal Shrike
Brubru
Puffback *(Southern Puffback)*
Threestreaked Tchagra *(Brownheaded Tchagra)*
Blackcrowned Tchagra
Tropical Boubou
Orangebreasted Bush Shrike
Greyheaded Bush Shrike
White Helmetshrike
Red-billed Helmetshrike *(Retz's Red-billed Helmet Shrike)*
Yellowspotted Nicator *(White-throated Nicator)*

DRONGOS, CROWS & RAVENS
Forktailed Drongo
Pied Crow
Whitenecked Raven

STARLINGS & OXPECKERS
Greater Blue-eared Starling
Leaser Blue-eared Starling
Longtailed Starling *(Southern Long-tailed Starling)*
Plumcoloured Starling *(Violet-backed Starling)*
White-winged Starling
Wattled Starling
Yellowbilled Oxpecker
Redbilled Oxpecker

SPARROWS, WEAVERS & QUELEAS
House Sparrow
Greyheaded Sparrow
Southern Grey-headed Sparrow
Yellowthroated Sparrow *(Yellow-throated Petronia)*
Red-billed Buffalo Weaver
Whitebrowed Sparrow-weaver
Chestnut-mantled Sparrow-weaver
Spectacled Weaver
Golden Weaver *(Large Golden Weaver)*
Lesser Masked Weaver
Masked Weaver *(African Masked Weaver)*
Spottedbacked Weaver *(Village Weaver)*
Redheaded Weaver
Cardinal Quelea
Redheaded Quelea
Redbilled Quelea

WAXBILLS & FIREFINCHES
Melba Finch
Goldenbacked Pytilia *(Orange-winged Pytilia)*
Redthroated Twinspot
Redbilled Firefinch
Jameson's Firefinch
Common Waxbill
Blue Waxbill
Orangebreasted Waxbill *(Zebra Waxbill)*
Bronze Mannikin
Pied Mannikin *(Magpie Martnikin)*
Cutthroat Finch

WIDOWS, WIDOWFINCHES, WHYDAHS & BISHOPS
Firecrowned Bishop *(Black-winged Red Bishop)*
Red Bishop
Yellowrumped Widow *(Yellow Bishop)*
Whitewinged Widow *(White-winged Whydah)*
Redcollared Widow *(Red-collared Whydah)*
Cuckoo Weaver *(Parasitic Weaver)*
Steelblue Widowfinch *(Village Indigobird)*
Purple Widowfinch *(Dusky Indigobird)*
Green Indigobird
Pintailed Whydah *(Pin-tailed Widow)*
Paradise Whydah *(Long-tailed Paradise Widow)*
Broadtailed Paradise Whydah *(Broad-tailed Paradise Widow)*

CANARIES & BUNTINGS
Yelloweyed Canary *(Yellow-fronted Canary)*
Bully Canary
Stripe-breasted Seed-eater
Rock Bunting *(Cinnamon-breasted Rock Bunting)*
Golden-breasted Bunting
Cabanis's Bunting

APPENDIX III

Trees Checklist

PALM FAMILY (ARECACEAE)
Wild date palm *(Phoenix reclinata)*
Raffia palm *(Raphia farinifera)*
Borassus palm *(Borassus aethiopum)*
llala Palm *(Hyphaene petersiana)*

FIG FAMILY (MORACEAE)
Large-leaved rock fig *(Ficus abutilifolia)*
F. bubu
Common wild fig *(F. bussei)*
Sandpaper fig *(F. capreifolia)*
African rock fig *(F. glumosa)*
Red-leaved rock fig *(F. ingens)*
Common wild fig *(F. natalensis)*
Zanzibar fig *(F. sansibarica)*
Lowveld fig *(F. stuhlmannii)*
Sycamore fig *(F. sycomorus)*

SOUR PLUM FAMILY (OLACACEAE)
Large-fruited olax *(0/ax obtusifolia)*
Small sourplum *(Ximenia americana)*
Large sourplum *(X. caffra)*

CUSTARD APPLE FAMILY (ANNONACEAE)
Annona reticulata
Wild custard-apple *(A. senegalensis)*
Purple cluster-pear *(Cleistochlamys kirkii)*
Northern dwaba-berry *(Friesodielsia obovata)*
Green-apple *(Monodora junodii)*
Oval green-apple *(M. stenopetala)*

CAPER FAMILY (CAPPARACEAE)
Rough-leaved boscia *(Boscia angustifolia)*
Broad-leaved boscia *(B. mossambicensis)*
Willow-leaved boscia *(B. salicifolia)*
Large-flowered cadaba *(Cadaba kirkii)*
Three-finger bush *(Cladostemon kirkii)*
Bead-bean *(Maerua angolensis)*
Large-flowered maerua *(M. kirkii)*
Cucumber bush *(Thilachium africanum)*
CONNARACEAE
Short-pod *(Byrsocarpus orientalis)*

Cassia Family (CAESAIPINIOIDEAE)
Red Syringa *(Burkea africana)*
Mopane *(Colophospermum mopane)*
White bauhinia *(Bauhinia petersiana)*
Yellow tree bauhinia *(B. tomentosa)*
Brachystegia bussei
Mountain-acacia *(Brachystegia glaucescens)*
Blue-leaved brachystegia *(B. manga)*
Small-leaved brachystegia *(B. microphylla)*
False mufuti *(B. utilis)*
Tamarind *(Tamarindus indica)*
Pod Mahogany *(Afzelia quanzensis)*
Long-tail cassia *(Cassia abbreviata)*
Monkey pod *(C. petersiana)*
Camel's foot *(Piliostigma thonningii)*

HERNANDIACAE
Propeller tree *(Gyrocarpus americanus)*

MIMOSA FAMILY (MIMOSOIDEAE)
Monkey thorn *(Acacia galpinii)*
Red thorn *(A. gerrardii)*
Sweet thorn *(A. karoo)*
Black thorn *(A. mellifera)*
Knob-thorn *(A. nigrescens)*
Scented thorn *(A. nilotica)*
White thorn *(A. polyacantha)*
Splendid acacia *(A. robusta)*
Paperbark acacia *(A. sieberana)*
Umbrella thorn *(A. tortilis)*
Delagoa thorn *(A. welwitschii)*
Fever tree *(A. xanthophloea)*
Worm-cure albizia *(Albizia anthelmintica)*
Mountain albizia *(A. brevifolia)*
Lowveld albizia *(A. glaberrima)*
Sickle-leaved albizia *(A. harveyi)*
Many-stemmed albizia *(A. petersiana)*
Paperbark albizia *(A. tanganyicensis)*
Poison-pod albizia *(A. versicolor)*
Lowveld newtonia *(Newtonia hildebrandtii)*
Tree entada *(Entada abyssinica)*
Sand ash *(Xylia torreana)*

PEA FAMILY (PAPILIONOIDEAE)
Wild mango *(Cordyla africana)*
Snake bean (Swartzia madagascariensis)
Nyala tree *(Xanthocercis zambesiaca)*
False-teeth tree *(Aeshynomene elaphroxylon)*
Large-leaved dalbergia *(Dalbergia boehmii)*
African ebony *(D. melanoxylon)*
Mane-pod *(D. nyasae)*
Mukwa *(Pterocarpus angolensis)*
Round-leaved bloodwood *(P. rotundifolius)*
Lucky bean *(Erythrina abyssinica)*
Broad-leaved erythrina *(E. latissima)*
Aloe erythrina *(E. livingstoniana)*
Narrow lance-pod *(Loncbocarpus bussei)*
Rain tree *(I. capassa)*
Wing pod *(Xeroderris stuhlmannii)*
Lesser millettia *(Millettia usaramensis)*
Cork bush *(Mundulea sericea)*
River bean *(Sesbania sesban)*
Small caterpillar pod *(Ormocarpum kirkii)*
Large caterpillar pod *(0. trichocarpum)*
Afrormosia *(Pericopsis angolensis)*

BALANITACEAE
Simple-thorned torchwood *(Balanites aegyptiaca)*
Torchwood *(B. maughamii)*
Small torchwood *(B. pedicellaris)*

CITRUS FAMILY (RUTACEAE)
Wild citrus *(Citropsis daweana)*
Oval-fruited teclea *(Teclea myrei)*
Rare woodland vepris *(Vepris zambesiaca)*
Knobwood *(Zanthozylum chalybeum)*
Sand knobwood *(Z. leprieurii)*

SIMAROUBACEAE
White syringa (Kirkia accuminata)

MYRRH FAMILY (BURSERACEAE)
Poison-grub commiphora (Commiphora africana)
Rough-leaved commiphora (C. edulis)
Paperbark commiphora (C. marlothii)
Velvet commiphora (C. mollis)
Pepper-leaved commiphora (C. mossambicensis)
C. glandulosa

MAHOGANY FAMILY (MELLACEAE)
Red Mahogany (Khaya nyasica)
Wooden-banana (Entandrophragma caudatum)
Honeysuckle tree (Turraea robusta)

MILKWORT FAMILY (POLYGAIACEAE)
Violet tree (Securidaca longipedunculata)
Leaf-berry tree (Tapura fischeri)

EUPHORBIA FAMILY (EUPHORBL4CEAE)
Kudu-berry (Pseudolachnostylis maprouneifolia)
Tassel berry (Antidesma venosum)
Venda bead-string (Alchornea laxiflora)
Knobby bridelia (Bride/la chthartica)
Velvet bridelia (B. mollis)
Lavender croton (Croton gratissimus)
Fever-berry (C. megalobotrys)
Rough-leaved croton (C menyhartii)

Candelabra tree (Euphorbia ingens)
Red-flowered Euphorbia (B. lividiflora)
Rubber hedge euphorbia (E. tin4calli)
Hairy drypetes (Drypetes gerrardii)
Sand drypetes (D. mossambicensis)
Pawn-broker tree (Excoecaria bussei)
Heart-fruit (Hymenocardia acida)
Red heart-fruit (H. ulmoides)
Spurred phyllanthus (Phyllanthus engleri)
Woody-cushion pheasant-berry (P. kirkianus)
Potato bush (P. reticulatus)
Manketti tree (Ricinodendron rautanenii)
White-berry bush (Securinega virosa)
Synadenium molle

MANGO FAMILY (ANACARPIACEAE)
Manila (Sclerocarya birrea)
Long-live (Lannea discolor)
Small-leaved lannea (L. humilis)
False manila (Lannea schweinfunthii)
Tarberry (Ozoroa reticulata)
Spiny rhus (Rhus gueinzii)
CELASTRACEAE
Kooboo-berry (Cassine aethiopica)
Large-flowered maytenus (Maytenus putterlickoides)
Confetti tree (M. senegalensis)

LITCHI & SOAP-BERRY FAMILY (SAPLNDACEAE)
African allophylus (Allophylus africanus)
Lowveld allophylus (A. alnifolius)

Soap-berry (Deinbollia xanthocarpa)
River litchi (Lecaniodiscus fraxiniflius)
Velvet-fruited zanha (Zanha africana)

BUFFALO-THORN FAMILY (RHAMNACEAE)
Jujube (Ziziphus abyssinica)
Buffalo-thorn (Z. mucronata)
Small jujube (Z. pubescens)
Bird plum (Berchemia discolor)

JUTE FAMILY (TIUACEAE)
Bastard brandybush (Grewia bicolor)
Donkeyberry (G. flavescens)
Bastard silver raisin (G. inaequilatera)
Green-haired cross-berry (G. lepidopetala)
Gold-fruited grewia (G. micrantha)
Grey grewia (G. monticola)
Green-petalled cross-berry (G. stolzii)
G. trimcata

HIBISCUS & MALLOW FAMILY (MALVACEAE)
Prickly tree hibiscus (Hibiscus diversifolius)
Snot apple (Azanza garkeana)

BAOBAB FAMILY (BOMBACACEAE)
Baobab (Adansonia digitata)

CACAO FAMILY (STERCULIACEAE)
Dombeya acutanguli
River dombeya (D. kirkii)
Wild pear (D. rotundifolia)

Tick tree (Sterculia africana)
Tall sterculia (S. appendiculata)
Large-leaved sterculia (S. quinqueloba)

OCHNA FAMILY (OCHNACEAE)
Large-leave ochna (Ochna gambleoides)
Closed-fruit ochna (0. rovumensis)
Brick-red ochna (0. scbweinfurthiana)

St John's wort family (CLUSIACEAE)
African mangosteen (Garcinia livingstonet)
Christmas berry (Psorosperrnum febrifugum)

KEI-APPLE FAMILY (FLACOURTIACEAE)
Fried-egg flower (Oncoba spinosa)
Kei-apple (Dovyalis caffra)
Bristly dovyalis (D. hispidula)
Flacourtia (Flacourtia indica)
Lindackeria sp

COMBRETUM FAMILY (COMBRETACEAE)
Redbushwillow (Combretum apiculatum)
Savanna bushwillow (C. celastroides)
Bushwilow (C. collinum)
Four-leaved combretum (C. fragrans)
Leadwood (C. lmberbe)
Velvet bushwillow (C. molle)
Shaving-brush combretum (C. mossambicense)
Thicket combretum (C. padoides)Large-

fruited combretum (*C. zeyheri*)
Two-winged pteleopsis (*Pteleopsis myrtifolia*)
River terminalia (*Terminalia sambesiaca*)
Silver terminalia (*T. sericea*)
Rosette-leaved terminalia (*T. stenostachya*)
Zig-zag terminalia (*T. stuhlmannii*)

IVY & CUSSONIA FAMILY (ARALIACEAE)
Octopus cabbage tree (*Cussonia arborea*)
Parsnip tree (*Heteromorpha trifoliata*)
Carrot tree (*Steganotaenia araliacea*)

STAMVRUG FAMILY (SAPOTACEAE)
Lowveld milkberry (*Manikara mochisia*)

EBONY FAMILY (EBENACEAE)
Pink diospyros (*Diospyros kirkii*)
African ebony (*D. mespiliformis*)
Crocodile-bark diospyros (*C. quiloensis*)
Peeling-bark diospyros (*D. senensis*)
Rigis-star berry (*D. squarrosa*)
D. truncatifolea

OLIVE FAMILY (OLEACEAE)
Wooden-pear (*Schrebera thichoclada*)

MUSTARD TREE FAMILY (SAILVADORACEAE)
Needle bush (*Azima tetracantha*)
Mustard tree (*Salvadora persica*)

Strychnos family (*LOGANIACEAE*)
Cape teak (*Strycbnos decussata*)
Dull-leaved mukwakwa (*S. innocua*)
Black monkey orange (*S. madagascarensis*)
Grape strychnos (*S. potatorum*)
Spiny monkey orange (*S. spinosa*)

OLEANDER FAMILY (APOCYNACEAE)
Jasmine tree (*Holarrhena pubescens*)
Wild rubber tree (*Diplorhynchus condylocarpon*)
Toad tree (*Tabernaemontana elegans*)
Quinine tree (*Rauvolfia caffra*)
Sabi star (*Adenium multiflorum*)

HELIOTROPE & FORGET-ME-NOT FAMILY (BORAGINACEAE)
Large-leaved cordia (*Cordia africana*)
Blue-bark cordia (*C. goetzei*)
Woolly cordia (*C. pilosissima*)
Sandpaper bush (*Ehretia amoena*)
Forest stamperwood (*E. cymosa*)

VERBENA FAMILY (VERBENACEAE)
Large-fruited vitex (*Vitex amboniensis*)
Orange-fruited vitex (*V. buchananii*)
Black plum (*V. doniana*)
Smelly-berry vitex (*V. mombassae*)
Chocolate berry (*V. payos*)
White cat's whiskers (*Clerodendrum glabrum*)
Blue cat's whiskers (*C. myricoides*)
Wild Chinese hats (*Holmskioldia tettensis*)

Northern premna (*Premna senensis*)

JACARANDA FAMILY (BIGNONIACEAE)
Bean tree (*Markhamia acuminata*)
Golden bean tree (*M. obtusifolia*)
M. zanzibarica
Pink jacaranda (*Stereospermum kunthianum*)
Fernandoa (*Fernandoa magnifica*)
Sausage tree (*Kigelia africana*)
Yellow elder (Tecoma stans)

GARDENIA FAMILY (RUBLACEAE)
Canthium crassum
Pink-fruited canthium (*C. frangula*)
C. pseudorandii
C. racenulosum
Cuviera semseii
Feritia (*Feretia aeruginescens*)
Large-leaved common gardenia (*Gardenia jovis-tonamtis*)
Gummy gardenie (*G. resiniflua*)
Comon gardenia (*G. bolkensii*)
Small false gardenia (*Geinsia crinita*)
Firebush (*Hymenodictyon floribundum*)
Yellow firebush (*H. parvifolium*)
Crystal-bark (*Crossopteryx febrifuga*)
Matumi (*Breonadia microcephala*)
Poison pavetta (*Pavetta schumanniana*)
Phyellocalyz rollesenii
Psydrax livida
P. martini
Wild medla (*Vangueria infausta*)
Rytigynia umbellulata

Trycalysia junodii

DAISY & THISTLE FAMILY (COMPOSITAE)
Tree vernoia (*Vernonia amygdalina*)
Star-flowered tree vernonia (V. colorata)

APPENDIX IV

Words
NJC   *Norman Joseph Carr.*
Dambo   *Marshy or swampy area*
Kakuli   *Lone buffalo bull.*